The Spirit's Self-Help Book

7 Spirits, 7 Stories
7 Songs for the Gypsy

Glenn Poveromo

Legwork Team Publishing
New York

AuthorHouse™
1663 Liberty Drive, Suite 200
Bloomington, IN 47403
www.authorhouse.com
Phone: 1-800-839-8640

© 2008 Glenn Poveromo

No part of this book may be reproduced, stored in a retrieval system, or transmitted by any means without the written permission of the author.

First published by AuthorHouse 1/28/08

ISBN: 978-1-4343-5648-2 (sc)

Legwork Team Publishing

Cover design, interior layout,
and print ready file by Legwork Team Publishing

Printed in the United States of America
Bloomington, Indiana

This book is printed on acid-free paper.

Dedication

This book is dedicated to those enlightened souls who understand the value of shining their light for the good of all of creation, and for those souls who are seeking to find their light within them. May your hearts and souls help in creating an energy of peace and love; may you help in creating a collective consciousness that fosters an energy of healing and harmony in our world.

Wishing you Peace, Love & a Smile in your Heart!

For the Gypsy

Contents

Prologue..10

Acknowledgments..12

Billy Smalls: The Possibility of a Parallel Universe....15
  Songs:
    My Best Friend..24
    When You Love Someone..................................26
    I Wish You Love..48
    Winds Of Change..61
    In My Heart I Can Hold You.............................63
    Gypsy Girl..78
    Billy Loves Haddie...83

The Chief: Life as an Individual Journey...................85

Mamma Soul: Rightful Thinking.............................109

Haitukulu: Matters of Soul......................................125

Angel of Zarton: Soul as Creator.............................145

Anisha: Soul Mates and Twin Flames.....................162

Ihon: Souls as Angels..189

Glennisms...209

Author's Note...212

Purchase Information Page.....................................214

Prologue

I have been offered a very unique and exciting opportunity. Seven spirits of the universe have contacted me and asked me to share their insights with you. Our souls are complex and contain many different components that allow us to contribute to the good of all of creation. These spirits have come forward to remind us that we too are spiritual beings, that we too should focus our attention on the essence of our being, which is our eternal soul.

I must admit that this is not a work of fiction. It is an actual communication with these spirits. I am not the author this work; I am merely the vehicle through which the spirits have chosen to express themselves. This compilation offers an opportunity to consider the possibility that spirits truly exist, and perhaps to expand your awareness of the boundless entities and energies that dwell in tandem with our human existence. Whatever your preconceptions, you will most likely be left with the question, "Why not?" resounding in your consciousness. There is a part in every soul that at least considers the possibility of a higher power and cosmic energy. Meeting these entities will, hopefully, not only be an entertaining experience but a revelation of truth as well.

I do not claim to be an authority on the inner workings of the universe. I am merely the conduit through which seven unique and genuine spirits have chosen to manifest themselves. The process of scribing their stories has been exhausting at times, but never tedious. Meeting each has been a most remarkable experience.

The facet that amazes me most about this endeavor is that the spirits have come forward with more than just an expression of their insights. They all come with their own songs as well. However, the first spirit is the one who asked that his "Songs for the Gypsy" be presented to you. I have honored his request and offered him the stage, which is a very comfortable and familiar place for him.

I have been given an incredible gift in being chosen to bring this work forward. I am grateful to the universe for choosing me to undertake this extraordinary project. I offer sincere thanks and appreciation. It is my deepest hope that you will enjoy meeting these spirits and will garnish the helpful insights they have chosen to reveal. May enlightenment fill your soul!

Acknowledgments

So many people have helped me to bring this work forward to the world. I have so many wonderful people to thank! First and foremost is my beautiful wife, Sheri, who has shared life with me as my true friend for thirty-three years. I thank you, Sheri, for your constant love, support, and inspiration. Thank you for allowing me to dream so many dreams and for always encouraging me to find ways to make them come true. Your love has helped me to understand the true power of love.

I also thank my daughter, Jessie, her husband, Tristan, and my son, Toby. Sharing love with you has kept my heart open to our true reason for living, which I believe is love itself.

I wish to thank my wonderful parents, Francelia and Louis Poveromo, for placing my feet on the path of understanding spirit. You opened my eyes to the world of possibility not by the words you spoke, but by the actions you modeled for us all. I love you!

I thank my sisters, Helen and Tina, and my niece, Kristin, for sharing with me their experiences of encounters with spiritual entities; you have all helped me to understand their reality.

My heart is filled with the joy of thanking Ms. Samantha Kifer, whose beautiful illustrations of the gypsy grace the pages of this book. I have known you since the day of your birth Sammie and watching you grow into the beautiful and special young lady that you are makes me smile. What a special treat to have your talent touch these pages. I love you!

I offer my sincere thanks to the many friends who have shared life with me in a special way. Your inspiration and friendship have helped to make my life an incredible journey of security and love. There are far too many to name, and my fear of omitting any of you by accident causes me to say a collective thank you to all—you know who you are!

A very special thanks is offered to my true friends from In the Wings Spiritual Book Club. It was your enthusiasm and kind words that gave me the push I needed to take this to the publisher. Sharing insights with you is my favorite day of each month. Blessing to you all!

I extend a special thanks to Terri Haupt. Proprietor of At The Corner Candles & Gifts in Lindenhurst, NY. I am among the many you graciously help each and every day. Love and gratitude to you and Tom.

Another special thank you is extended to my cousin John "Butch" Poveromo for his generous help in working on Billy Smalls's songs. I've enjoyed sharing special time with you and Janine. Thanks Butch, you are a great cousin and an even greater friend.

I extend a special thank you to my buddy Bobby Begun for all your help with the photos. You and Mary are loved so much!

I also wish to thank all of the wonderful teachers and staff members who have worked with me in the Wantagh School District during my career as a teacher. I have admired you all for the true caring you brought to our students. You should all be recognized for the selfless ways you've touched the lives of so many children. My gratitude and respect for you is immeasurable.

My heartfelt thanks are offered to the thousands of students and athletes that have been my heart and soul for so many years. You have offered me such an incredible privilege in being a part of your life. I remember each and every one of you in a special way, for each of you has touched my life in a special way. It is from you I learned so many of life's lessons. I honestly cannot recall a day in thirty-five years that I did not smile at least one smile. It is because of you I whispered to myself each day that I was not going to work, I was going to love.

Finally, I offer my sincere thanks to those spirits who have come forward to share their valuable insights with you all. Thank you for choosing me to be the vehicle through which your valuable advice is rendered. *Soo-nah-mahnte, soo-nah-mhey...*

Billy Smalls
The Possibility of a Parallel Universe

Billy Smalls is a spirit who has chosen to come forward and share his story with you. Billy is a bit of an enigma to me, for I've not yet come to understand if he is an entity living on a parallel plane or if he is an entity who has presented himself as a fictional character with a message to us all regarding the inner workings of spirit. However, through his insights he wishes to enrich your life in some way; he wishes to offer you the concept that we are all eternal souls.

Billy has asked to tell his story because he believes that you might better understand your own spirit by relating to the "humanness" of his character as he reveals his unique and interesting tale. His story is both human and cosmic simultaneously, for Billy is a true spirit who is living the human condition at a frequency of vibration different from you and me. You are being asked to consider that all things are possible through spirit, for so much of this vibration exists beyond the five senses that are familiar to us.

The notion of parallel universes suggested by quantum physics may indeed explain Billy's existence. Although Billy exists as a fictional character on this earthly plane as we know it, his presence and spirit are as genuine as yours and mine. His life and vibration are the creation of his own free will. Perhaps by reading his story you will understand the concept that we too are spirits and free to choose our perceptions and incarnations through our own free will. Perhaps you will understand that our thoughts and belief systems shape our reality, which empowers us to perceive life however we choose. It is Billy's hope that you will.

As his story unfolds, you will come to know Billy by more than his public persona. He appears to be somewhat of a vagabond. He is a man of music who, for years, has made his way around the country and the world by playing his guitar and enjoying intimate moments with numerous women, yet all the while sharing his soul with only one—his twin flame and the true love of his life. He is difficult for anyone to know, not only because of his extensive travels, but also because he is a private man and not particularly conversant with the public at large. His elusive charm is a large part of his alluring mystique.

When I began my interview with Billy, he was seated comfortably on his aged recliner, which had been part of the original décor of his New York, West Side co-op since the first day he moved in. He looked very relaxed in his blue cotton jeans, white silk shirt, black leather vest, and his ever-present black Stetson hat with gold trim. His graying hair was tied back into a ponytail, giving him the look of a rugged cowboy. It was easy to see why this man had so many tales to tell, for

Billy Smalls

his eyes exuded a wise, yet youthful, charm that I recognized as being irresistible. When he moved his chair into its reclined position, I understood the interview was about to begin.

* * *

The Spirit's Self-Help Book

G: Well, Billy, I must say I am eager and honored to be here at this moment. I want to thank you for coming forward as the first of numerous spirits who have asked to reveal their special insights.

Billy: My pleasure, G. It's about time, really.

G: About time?

Billy: Yeah, about time. You should have started this years ago.

G: Probably so. But this is not about me; it's about you. The story goes that you really began your adventure, as you call life, at the age of sixteen. Would you elaborate on this statement?

Billy: Yeah, sure. But my story actually begins from my childhood. You see, I grew up in a place called Lindenhurst, Long Island, which is in the state of New York. It's a great state in the USA. I was the fourth of six kids. I have two brothers and three sisters. We lived in a modest four-bedroom Cape Cod house. It was cramped and crowded and often hectic, but it was okay. It wasn't different from any other households in our community. My father was a good man, although I barely got to know him. He worked six days a week in a factory where they made parts for airplanes. I really didn't spend too much time with him because he always seemed to be working. It bothered me a lot, not so much because of the time he spent at work—most of us had dads who worked long hours—it was just that

I sensed he was a very intelligent man, more intelligent than the other men I saw around me. As a kid I could never figure out why a man of his intelligence worked himself into a grave in some crowded factory, doing very unskilled and repetitive work. I now know why it was so, but I didn't back then. That's something to tell at another time. But anyway, he died when I was twelve. He suffered a massive heart attack.

His passing was tough on our family. People in our community weren't big on insurance policies back in those days, so our family was left in kind of a mess. With six kids and a modest income, there wasn't a whole lot of money around. Mom had never worked; that was the way it was in those old blue-collar communities back then. She eventually got a job in the church rectory as a receptionist, cook, cleaner. I guess working around priests eased her spirit a bit. Anyway, the rest of us were supposed to get jobs to help support our family. There was plenty for kids to do in those days. You could have a paper route, work in a supermarket, or labor for someone's dad. I tried the paper route gig. It was okay. I delivered papers for Newsday. I had fifty-two papers on my route and brought in about forty bucks a week, which was decent money at that time. My customers all knew my family situation and were generous with their tips.

After my dad passed, I felt kind of lonely. Even though I didn't spend much time with him, I loved him with all my heart. He was my dad, and he was my hero. I'd listen to anything he told me. Once in a while we'd go fishing on a Sunday, just him and me. I've been on trips, tours, and vacations all over the world in my lifetime, but nothing can ever match just sitting on the dock of the Great South Bay and being with my dad. He was the best man I've ever known, even to this day. He was simply the best.

When he passed I didn't know how to talk to anyone about it, so I became kind of antisocial. Good thing there weren't any drugs around my community in those days because I definitely would have gotten caught up in that life.

The thing that saved my life at that time was music. One of my customers was moving away, and before they left they gave me this old guitar. It wasn't much of an instrument, but it became my best companion. I spent hours with that thing, literally hours on end. I never had a lesson. I couldn't afford that. I knew this older guy named Nelson who played, and he showed me some basic chords and a couple of cool techniques, and the rest I learned myself. By the time I was sixteen, I was playing pretty good. That's when I decided to make my move. That's when I left home.

I use the word *left* rather than *ran away* because that's the way it was. I could see what was happening in my home. I would probably have to work small jobs for the rest of my life just to keep up with the bills and so forth. I would be doing the same thing my dad did, and I did not want that for myself. So I figured I might as well get out of town before the mold was cast and that kind of life became permanent. I went to my mom and told her how I felt and that I was going to leave. Of course she objected and tried to talk me out of it, but she couldn't. In my mind I was going, and that was it. She would have one less mouth to feed and I would be moving far away from the factory mentality.

Billy Smalls

G: You were sixteen and just up and left? What about school? Where did you go?

Billy: School was no problem. I just wasn't going back. Simple. Where I wound up was New York City. In my mind I was going to play music for a living. I knew from listening to the radio that there was plenty of music action in the city. There was a big folk music movement going on at the time, so I headed for Greenwich Village. Of course things didn't go as planned at first. I had no money, except for a small bankroll from the paper route, and no place to go. Fortunately I arrived at the end of the summer so all the nights I had to sleep outside weren't too bad. I hung around all the coffeehouses and any street where musicians were hanging out and playing. I eventually hooked up with these three guys, and we formed a band. The Wingers, we called ourselves. We played a lot of Dylan and Phil Oaks type of stuff. We were okay, but nothing special. But that little band is what changed my life in so many ways. It was because of that one gig we played that I met Haddie McDowell. At first I thought it was just a weird accident, but now I realize it was fate. Haddie changed and saved my life. She was the greatest and most exciting thing that has ever happened to my life, even to this day.

G: I know she's been very special to you. Just how did you meet, and exactly what developed between you?

Billy: That's a great question and a great memory. You see, one night we were playing in some crummy little club down on West 3rd St. We weren't exactly headliners so we didn't get to play the good places. Anyway, after we finished our last set, this incredibly beautiful woman came up to me and said hi. She told me how much she liked the way I played and asked if she could buy me a drink. I didn't even drink at that time, it was not yet a part of my lifestyle, but I said sure. I didn't even know what to order. She knew I was feeling awkward, but she was cool about it. She smiled and told me not to worry about a thing. She brought me back a scotch, my first ever. It was the beginning of so many "first evers" from that point on.

To make a long story short, that was the night my life began. Haddie took me right here to this very apartment in which we're sitting. We made love right over there on that couch. She was amazing; she knew I was a virgin and that the first time was so important. She was gentle, assertive, considerate, and oh, so wild!

G: That's a good story, but it went too fast. Could you explain a bit more about Haddie and her attraction to you?

Billy: Okay, but it will take awhile to tell.

G: I have time. I'd love to hear it.

Billy: Well, I know you have quite a few others to interview, but if you want to hear it I'll tell you.

Haddie was married to William McDowell, who was a major player on Wall Street. He came from a family loaded with money. His father was a business associate of the biggest players on the New York Stock Exchange, so you can imagine the money that was involved. William and his three brothers were all moguls on the exchange, all very rich and savvy kinds of guys. Haddie came from a family of wealth also. Her roots were from her grandfather's success in the garment industry. Anyway, you know how it goes. Money marries money. It's just the way it is.

Haddie was a society girl through family and marriage, but she wasn't that way inside. She was actually more of a street kind of person in her soul. Sure, she was bred in the traditions of wealth. She knew the right things to do and say. But she would always manage to sneak away to the other side of the tracks, so to speak. As a young woman she loved parties, music, dancing, drinking, laughing loudly, and wild sexual adventures. It was just her nature to be that way. She still is to a certain degree, although age has mellowed her quite a bit.

Anyway, when I met Haddie she was thirty-one and properly married. She did her partying but had cut out her sexual escapades. She had been true to her vows of fidelity. However, she didn't spend lots of time with her husband. He was always busy, always traveling. He had so much money, he really couldn't spend it all if he tried. They owned homes literally all over the world. They traveled together a lot, but he also traveled alone quite a bit. Haddie always suspected that he had affairs all over the place. At first she handled it okay. She loved him. He was good to her, treated her well. But things change sometimes. She got tired of suppressing her sexual desires, especially when she knew in her heart that old William was not doing the same. So that's how we came to meet. I just happened to be playing the night she decided to liberate herself. Neither one of us realized what would come of it. It turned out to be a lifelong relationship.

G: You are still together today?

Billy: Yes we are. Haddie and I are an eternal team. She's remained the best friend I've ever had, or will ever have, for that matter.

My Best Friend

Well I'd like to find a way,
for my grateful heart to say
Thank you for being my best friend
Well we'll always be together;
it will be that way forever
You and me living life as best friends
Thank you, my friend,
thank you for being my very best friend

Well sometimes my thoughts get hazy,
but you never think I'm crazy
You just help to chase those clouds away
And any time I feel like crying,
it's on you I'll be relying
Help me through and find a brighter day
Thank you, my friend,
thank you for being my very best friend

And if I sail through troubled waters,
I'll have a wise and faithful guide
I'll find a safe and peaceful harbor
With my best friend traveling by my side

Billy Smalls

Well sometimes my legs get weary,
that's the time I need you near me,
You give me strength to stand up tall on my own
And in the middle of a cold dark night,
well I'll seek your shining light,
Thoughts of you will bring me safely back home
Thank you, my friend,
well I thank you for being my very best friend

I want to share your joy and laughter,
help you live happily thereafter
Well your smile just fills up all of my soul
And any time you need me near you,
call my name you know I'll hear you
I'll be there to help you feel safe and whole
Thank you, my friend,
thank you for being my very best friend…

G: So, tell me more about your early years with Haddie.

Billy: They were great. See, she chose me, knowing I was so young and all, to be her lover. She said it was something that just rushed through her when she saw me playing up on the stage. She could see I was a minor and all, but that didn't stop her from doing what she did. She said it was just a feeling, so strong she had to act on it. Anyway, from that night on we became a team. This place was one of her spare refuges. Rich people do that a lot. She owned it as her little getaway. She hadn't used it for sex with anyone; I already told you that she had no infidelities at the time. But she liked to slip away from her high society world for a day or two when her husband was away.

Well, needless to say I became quite intoxicated by that woman. Try being a teenager and introduced to sex by an incredibly beautiful, incredibly wild, incredibly rich, and incredibly intelligent woman who is twice your age. I didn't have a chance. I fell in love in the middle of the very first kiss. Haddie was cool though, she understood just how I would be feeling, and she spent a lot of time helping me understand that I was really in lust, not in love. She helped me understand so many things. She was my teacher, as well as my lover and best friend. In time I truly did come to love her, and she loved me.

When You Love Someone

When you love someone you want to hold them in your arms, every day and every night
When you love someone you look into their eyes and whisper words of love beneath the pale moonlight
When you love someone they're always on your mind no matter what you do
Well there's someone that I love, the one I really love
The someone who I love is you

When you love someone there's music in the air and you hear it everywhere you go
When you love someone you feel it deep inside, it's a feeling you can't hide and you're all aglow
When you love someone they're always by your side in everything you do

Billy Smalls

Well there's someone that I love, the one I really love
The someone who I love is you

I want to journey through life with you forever
I want to walk always close by your side
I want to lay next to you beneath a blanket of stars
I want to fill your every day with sunny skies

When you love someone you hear your favorite song,
you start to sing along and you smile so bright
When you love someone there's magic in the air and you feel
it everywhere both day and night
When you love someone you know deep in your heart that
you always will be true
Well there's someone that I love, the one I really love
The someone who I love is you

I want to spend every day with you in heaven
I want to make the sweetest love to you each night
I want to lay you down in sheets of fine white satin
I want to fill your heart and soul with love's delight

When you love someone you listen
oh so close to every word they say
When you love someone the thrill of their embrace will make
your spirit soar and take you far away
When you love someone it feels like
all of life is beautiful and new
Well there's someone that I love, the one I really love
The someone who I love is you…

G: That must have been quite an exciting time in your life. Just how did you manage to advance your musical abilities during that period? How did you survive financially and so forth?

Billy: That was easy—Haddie took care of all of that. She gave me a roof over my head, money in my pocket, and food on my table. She gave me everything. She even hooked me up with the best guitar teachers in the city. I had studio time whenever I wanted it, musicians to play with, the whole nine yards.

Now, it will seem to anyone reading this that I was a spoiled kid, a real user. At least that's what I would think if I were reading it. But it wasn't that way, really. See, it was a bit confusing for me at first. Even though I was getting a free ride, I wasn't real comfortable about it. Don't forget my roots. My dad worked so hard all his life. I knew what that was about. I was having a real problem dealing with getting things for free. But like everything else, Haddie saw the problem and explained how to handle it. She offered me perspectives that were so foreign to me but, when I took the time to consider them, they began to make sense.

G: You mean she helped you feel good about your situation?

Billy: Yes, she did. See, Haddie saw right into my soul. It was as if she could read my mind. She explained to me that I should feel good about the way she was taking care of me, for a few reasons. The first was that I was actually taking care of her. It was very difficult for her to live in the world in which she did. She was a proper society woman, as I mentioned before, but she had this burning desire to live apart from that world. We found out many years later the reason why. It wasn't until she was in her forties that she discovered she was adopted. She was the illegitimate child of a wealthy politician. Her mother was a gypsy. It's a very long story and a very interesting one as well. But that's for later.

Anyway, the way Haddie explained it, I was really providing for her. I gave her a chance to live a part of her life through her soul. As far as the money was concerned, it wasn't significant to her at all. She and her husband had so much of it that what she provided for me was what she called "a mere pittance." She said the pleasure I provided for her was worth more than a ton of gold. I knew she meant it and that was a lesson I learned at an early age. The lesson is that many times by receiving, you are actually giving. The difference is the way you receive. If it's with love and good intention, then you are giving. If it's with indifference and selfish intentions, then it's a sin.

The next perception she brought to my consciousness was that we were linked very closely in our souls. We now realize that we both have some gypsy blood in our veins. Although there is quite a gap in our ages, our spirits are linked as one. I thought it took a lot of courage for her to approach me that first night—it must have been awkward for a woman in her thirties to come on to a teenager—but Haddie explained that she had no choice. Her soul exploded when she saw me, and she knew. A voice inside of her just called out that she had found her twin flame, the completion of her soul. That was all there was to it. Through that lesson I've learned there really is no finite time in

The Spirit's Self-Help Book

the universe. Sure, life in one incarnation at a time is finite, but that's like a school year or a season in a sport. There's always next fall, always next season, always next lifetime.

Haddie also convinced me that my job at that time was to become the best musician I possibly could be. Of course, I was into a real party mode in the beginning. Wouldn't you be? I mean, one minute I'm away from home, sleeping on the street, and the next I'm living like the Duke of Earl. Great place to live, great connections, great music, great woman, great sex, great friend. Great, great, great! How many people really get to be like Cinderella? I did, and it took a while to calm my ego down. But Haddie was patient, and it didn't take as long as you might suspect for me to stop being filled with myself. By my eighteenth birthday I was thinking maturely for someone my age. I wasn't exactly a man of the world, but I did have the advantage of seeing life through the eyes of someone much older than myself. When I reflect on that period of my life, I realize just how wonderful it was. It's embedded so deeply in my soul. Wow!

G: It sounds like paradise to me. You certainly were not the average American teenager. You were a long way from Wally and The Beaver! Tell me, though, did your whole life run smoothly after you hooked up with Haddie? Were there any rough spots to deal with?

Billy: Yeah, there were some real lessons to learn.

G: What was your first lesson, as you describe it?

Billy: My first lesson is that life doesn't stay the same, even when it does. What I mean by that is you can be in the same place with the same people for thirty years and things will be different.

Haddie and I weren't together for more than a couple of years when things began to change a little. See, when I was about nineteen I figured I was mature beyond my years and I was ready to marry Haddie. As usual, she understood my feelings but kept insisting that my outlook would change. She told me that I needed to get out and see the world on my own a bit, find out about myself and what was going on beyond my own existence. I didn't want to hear that, though. As far as I was concerned, it was Haddie and me forever. By this time in our relationship, we began to acknowledge that love had developed between us. I just figured that if we loved each other, it would be enough to sustain us forever. Haddie tried to explain that our world, as we knew it, made it easy for us to express our love, but if we went out on our own, things would be quite different. I understand that now, but at the time I simply could not see it.

The other thing that really was getting me was the fact that she had deep feelings for William. That really drove me wild.

G: She loved you both at once?

Billy: Yeah, she did. Only she loved us differently. I gave her passion. I gave her dreams. William gave her a good life and friendship. I couldn't understand or accept it at that particular time, but now I can see that what she had with William was a beautiful relationship in its own way, as was ours. But it hurt when she left me and went back to her husband. It hurt so bad.

G: She left you? Could you explain?

Billy: William became ill. He was diagnosed with prostate cancer. In those days that was a lot more serious than it is today. As soon as Haddie found out, she became frantic. She told me she had to devote all her time and energy to help in finding a way to cure her husband. She had to devote all of her emotions to him to be able to do this in the best possible way. That meant putting our relationship on hold; she explained that in her heart she knew it was something she just had to do. I understood in a small way; I honestly did. But I couldn't accept the fact that she was leaving. She didn't abandon me though. Every few weeks money came in the mail, and occasionally she would phone. The calls stopped after a while because it always wound up by me getting irate and begging her to come back to me. I was very selfish at the time. I thought I was real mature, but in reality I was still a teenager. That's when I decided to leave. I was going to hit the road and find myself. That's just what I did.

G: You left? Where did you go and what did you do?

Billy: I gathered a group of musicians together and hit the road. Simple as that. It took a few weeks to find a groove. We began playing in small clubs, but in time we graduated to bigger and better places. The truth is we were pretty good. I had met and played with some pretty talented people during the years I spent in New York. I put together an ensemble of seven people, five guys and two girls. We called ourselves Top Gun. We were brassy, bold, and sexy. We lived hard and played hard. People were attracted to our style and our energy. It turned out to be a really great gig.

G: I'm assuming by the tone of your voice and the twinkle in your eye that you had a few adventures along the way.

Billy: Oh, lord, I certainly did. I went really wild for a while. It was so exciting, so exhilarating. Man, did I ever have a party!

G: Care to explain?

Billy: Well, you can imagine how it goes when you're young and the star, even in the small places. You're just a small star there, but a star just the same. The girls love you, and the guys want to be you. It kind of makes you feel free. You don't necessarily feel better than other people, just freer. And powerful. That feeling is what makes you attractive to so many women. I don't have to elaborate on how that went. Let's just say that I had very few nights when I went to bed alone, and when I did it was by choice. But those were the fringe benefits, really. The thing that was exciting me most was the music. I loved playing, I still do. I began to feel, and do to this day, that my dad's passing was a gift to me. Had he not died and left me alone, I might not have discovered music, at least not in the way I did.

Anyway, life in those days was great. We traveled constantly. We didn't make lots of money and didn't stay in the best places. In fact, some nights were spent in our vans. But that didn't matter. At that time all we wanted to do was enjoy life. We traveled so much. Initially we went down the Eastern Seaboard. We did Jersey, Philly, Baltimore, and a bunch of places in Virginia. We kept going south but didn't do too well in the country places. After our second gig in Georgia we decided to keep going south. We got our butts kicked by a tribe of rednecks in a place called Bubba Jack's Roadhouse. After that we went straight to Fort Lauderdale and the Keys. Those were great gigs. We stayed in Florida for almost two years. There was so much action there. Constant bookings, incredibly beautiful women, late nights, and unfortunately, drugs galore. That was the beginning of some very productive, yet very hard times for me and a few others in the band.

G: Productive and hard? Please explain.

Billy: Well, musically it was great. We were so tight by this time, it was incredible. We had begun as a cover band but gradually we began to write our own material. Our original stuff was catching on, and we were approached by one of the major labels. They offered us a pretty sweet deal, which included money, recording, and first class travel. No more carting all our stuff around and sleeping wherever. A tour bus and roadies were very appealing. We had to put together an album of songs and get the show on the road. We attacked the hell out of that opportunity.

Billy Smalls

We had a great time in that studio. Lots of long hours of playing, lots of fantastic women hanging around and then, lots of booze and drugs. Sounds like a typical rock story doesn't it? The truth is, that's just what it was.

Well, we put together a pretty good album. We called it *Soul of the Road*. It had kind of a theme about it, you know, songs which were stories about life on the road. Some were happy, some bluesy. We were pretty satisfied with the work we'd done, and the label got us on the air. We were received pretty well. Our first record got up to seventeen on the charts. Not a killer, but it was all right. We remained based in Fort Lauderdale for a while longer. Then when our second single "Bottom Line" was released, we went on our first official tour. It was basically a college gig. We headed north again. We did so many schools, from places like little Ellsworth College to places like Rutgers and Penn State. You might think that the big schools were the coolest, but that wasn't necessarily true. College kids were pretty much the same everywhere we played. If you liked rock music, then you liked rock music. Simple. Plus college campuses are cool because they're filled with kids who are busting to find and express themselves. It's a party time of life for most. Lots of exploring. Lots of everything. We were basically the same age and filled with the same energy, but we were the stars. You can imagine how we took advantage of that one.

During those days I began to develop a pretty bad drinking habit. It was hard to avoid, really. The life of a musician is very different from the life of people living by conventional standards. The hours are different, goals are different. Rockers tend to be hard livers. It's just part of the game. So many get caught up in the whole deal and eventually drink and drug themselves into oblivion. That should have been my story, except I had a safety net to catch me.

G: I'm guessing the safety net to which you're referring was Haddie?

Billy: Yeah, Haddie saved me. But not at first. I had to fall all the way to the bottom before I let her help me. It was about ten years before that happened.

G: Ten years is a very long time! How did that come to be, and what went on during those ten years?

Billy: Ten years seemed like forever. Especially at the end. I was desperate by that time. I thought I was going to die.
But before I go there I have to tell you how it evolved. See, we eventually made it as headliners. You remember our music, it seems like everyone does. It was great but it got old for me after a short while. As much success as I was having, as many women as I was hooking up with, there were two incredible pains in my soul, both the same in intensity.
One was that I was disappointing my dad. I would sometimes sit alone by the water and imagine him sitting next to me, looking at me with disappointed eyes. It wasn't because I was a musician; it was because of the way I was living. Too many drugs, too much alcohol, too much taking advantage of girls who were vulnerable. I was making my own money and paying my own bills, at least that's what I thought anyway. That's a story of its own. Anyway, the more I felt my dad's presence,

the more I drank and drugged, trying to chase his image away. The only time I felt secure was when I was blasted, so I stayed blasted most of the time.

The second pain I was experiencing was Haddie. I treated her so poorly for such a long time. I can't believe she stuck it out with me, continued to believe in me and support me. You see, I was so angry and hurt that she didn't want me, even though deep down I knew she did. I don't blame her for supporting her husband at the time she did. Not now at least. I realize it sounds so strange, our relationship and the things it required to succeed. Life is strange for us all. I grew up differently than most teens. My life was very unconventional. Most kids my age were preparing for college and future careers. I was rocking and sharing life with a mistress. It was wrong by conventional standards. I mean, you're supposed to love, honor, and obey one person. But it doesn't always work that way, and I don't believe it's wrong either. But that's for me, and it's my personal story. We all have our own personal stories. I judge no one for the way they think or live.

Anyway, I became very belligerent toward Haddie. I'd call once in a while, when I was buzzed off my butt, and brag to her about all my sexual escapades. I was hoping to hurt her and that she'd beg me to come home. But she never did and that drove me crazy. She would beg me to straighten myself out. She offered to pay for my rehab. But she wouldn't tell me not to be with other women. And she didn't offer to leave William. He was dying a slow death. I didn't really know it at the time, but that's what was happening. He was in remission for a few years, but Haddie had this way of knowing things. She knew he would slip back into cancer and it would take him from this earth. It was important for her to be faithful to him during his final years. I hated her and loved her for that, all in the same breath. But it only made me drink and drug harder. You know, success is a funny thing. At least what we perceive success to be. There I was, up on that stage, making great music, making lots of money. All the women, all the adulation, all the everything. You might think I was doing so great but you didn't see my pain. It was so deep, so incredible, and so constant. But I was always a kind of solitary man, even as a kid. I kept my troubles to myself. Through this whole thing I managed to maintain my skills as a musician, at least until the very end. So I was living great on the outside while fighting an incredible battle within myself every moment of the day.

G: That sounds awfully difficult. I, like most others, was not aware of what was taking place in your life. Did you ever consider rehab during those days? Did you want to clean yourself up?

Billy: I thought about it all the time after a while. But what happens is by the time you understand you have a problem, you're in it too deep. I didn't really realize the dependence I was developing when I first started out. I thought I could handle it. Ask anyone with a substance abuse problem. But what happens is that by the time you want to kick it, the demons are in control. That's what drugs and alcohol are. They're demons. They take you away from the way life is supposed to be lived. They tell you sweet lies and before you know it, they own you. They own your mind and if you let them, they'll own your soul. They definitely had my mind and almost took my soul.

Billy Smalls

G: How did you save your soul?

Billy: It was Haddie. She actually threw me down and beat me up, right on that couch over there. The next day I was in rehab. I've been drug free and sober ever since.

G: She threw you down and beat you up! Can you please go back to that one!

Billy: I knew you'd ask that. It sounds very strange, I know that. But that's what happened. She beat the hell out of me. Ten years of kindness and understanding had taken its toll on her. I needed my ass kicked and, lord, did she ever kick it!

See, down toward the end I was out of control. I was high twenty-four hours a day, and I had lost it. I stopped showing up for rehearsals and messed up on stage during the gigs. The band and management got tired of my ways. I wasn't a bastard when I was out of it, I was just withdrawn. I wouldn't tell anyone why I was doing what I was doing, and that frustrated them even more. For a long time everyone tried to be understanding and help me along, but after a while they got sick of babysitting. I was ruining a good thing, and enough was enough. At the end of a show in Boston, I got kicked out of the band. My manager was cool about it; he explained honestly why I was being let go. The sad thing is that I understood and internally agreed with him. He escorted me to the bus depot and put me on a Greyhound for New York. That was it. After ten years of building something so special, I had thrown it away. I had to ride a lousy bus in the middle of the night. I was gone and soon to be forgotten. Life works that way, you know.

You can be on top of the heap for as long as you can, but once you're gone, people forget you real quick. That's why no one should take himself too seriously. You're only as good as your last at bat. That's how people perceive you.

Well, the only place I had to go was right here where we're sitting. Haddie had maintained it for me through thick and thin. I didn't want to come here because I hated admitting to myself that I was a screw-up, and I wasn't particularly proud to be dependent on a wonderful woman who I had treated so poorly. Our relationship had deteriorated because of my selfish perceptions. But I was determined to live on my own. I didn't even call her to tell her I was here. I figured I had enough money to support myself and I would just chill for a while, then get a place of my own. I found out pretty quickly that plan wouldn't work. I found out I was broke.

G: You were broke? How in the world did that happen? How could someone who had become a superstar have nothing left? I don't understand.

Billy: Neither did I, at first anyway. I was in shock. But the truth is, I was broke. I had never taken the time to pay attention to my money. I had a money manager for that. I had never wanted for anything. All my expenses were always paid. Cash was not my way of living. All I ever did was sign my name. It might be difficult for the average working man to understand but my situation was different. Sure, I had access to cash whenever I needed it, but I rarely needed it. I would ask my manager about my investments and he would always tell me how great I was doing. I believed him. In retrospect I was a fool, a sucker, but hindsight is indeed twenty-twenty. I always thought robbers were mean, ugly-faced thugs. I learned they are sometimes your best friends, who sport the brightest smile. But the bottom line is, broke is broke, and that's what I was. Just plain broke.

Well, that was the straw that broke my back. I was now totally screwed up. I didn't have the strength or clarity of mind to initiate a lawsuit. I became a very bitter man. I had a decent stash of drugs and alcohol, and hit it hard every day. I never even left this apartment. To be honest, I can't recall too many details of those days and nights because they were a blur. I didn't even know that at that time William McDowell had passed into his next lifetime. I do know I lost touch with everything and everyone, except my pain. I was in an incredible depression. If you haven't experienced a state of mind like that, it's difficult to understand how it works. Even if you feel like you want to move, you can't. You lose all your personal power. Your mind grows weaker and winds up being deluded. I reached the point where I began to ponder suicide. It started out as a distant option, but each day it became more and more viable. It got to the point that I considered it my only way out. The part of you that tells you that you're crazy gives way to the part that tells you it's the world that's crazy and you don't belong in it. The demons were in control. They were standing right next to me and telling me to end it all. I became consumed by the concept and began plotting my death. It was just a matter of how I would go out. I did pray a couple of times that an angel would rescue me from my plight, but I never believed my prayer would be answered. I moved closer to death. I decided to OD on downers and booze. It was the least painful way to do it.

G: This is very difficult for me to believe. Did you actually go through with it? How were you saved?

Billy: Here's the part that most people won't believe, but that's okay because I believe it for myself. An angel did hear my prayer. You see, I was all set to go. I had a whole pile of reds and a bottle of Jack on that table over there. I planned to do it as soon as I wrote my suicide note. I felt I had to explain my truest feelings to Haddie before I cashed out. I wanted her to know how much I truly loved her, how much I admired and respected her, of how grateful I was for the ways she had helped me grow and experience life. I wanted to tell her how I carried her in my heart each minute of the day. Each and every day. I wanted to apologize for not revealing my feelings to her, how I had become a weak and insecure man. I wanted to ask her forgiveness. Without it I could never rest in peace. I finished writing the note and popped the first red into my mouth. I was going to take them one at a time. Just as I reached for the bottle of Jack, the door flew open. There were two wide eyes blazing right through me. It was Haddie.

Her glare froze me in that chair. We were both motionless for a moment, then all hell broke loose. She rushed right over to the table and grabbed the note. I sat very still as she read it. I guess I expected her to soften, break down and cry by the time she finished reading it. But she was not of the same mindset. When she finished reading it, she crumpled it in a ball and threw it in my face. She then grabbed the table and thrust it upward toward me. The booze and the pills went flying all over the place and I was knocked backward off my chair. She screamed at me, "You lousy, bastard! How dare you do this! How fucking dare you!" She then reached down and grabbed me by my hair and yanked me to my feet. We struggled for a moment as she forced me toward the couch. I was really too weak and startled to resist. She threw me on the couch and jumped on top of me, straddling me with her thighs. Then her fists began to fly. She began beating me all over the place—my face, my head, arms, chest, anywhere she could find an opening to strike. She was screaming like a wild banshee, calling me all kinds of names. She was not a very big woman in stature, but I suppose all those years of frustration gave her the strength of a lumberjack. I became so weak and overwhelmed by her fury that I could not fight back. I felt myself getting dizzy and the room becoming dark. I guess she could see I was ready to pass out, and that must have caused her rational mind to begin to take control. She was probably thinking she might be killing me. She jumped off me and began pacing around the room. Her fury was still raging through her but she had sense enough to stop the beating. She began ransacking my apartment, rummaging through the drawers until she found some twine. She came back to the couch and tied my wrists and feet, just in case I came to and tried to resist her. The whole time she was cursing me. I can't recall her exact words but I can recall her fury. I had no choice but to lay there and take it. The truth is I didn't want to resist her. I felt she was right. I was all the things she was calling me. But the thing that took me by surprise and what I'll always remember is the last thing she said before she broke down in tears. She said, "I'm not going to let the other man I love die too. I'm not going to let you die!"

I remember the tone of her voice—that sad, angry tone. I remember seeing her eyes well with tears and her chin tremble. I remember the resolve in her stare. Then I remember the darkness taking over.

G: You passed out? What happened after that!

Billy: I woke up in a hospital bed. Haddie saved my life.

G: That's an incredible story and I want to hear what happened in rehab. But before I go there, I'd like you to clarify something. When you began describing Haddie's intervention, you told me that you had asked an angel to help you and your prayer was answered. Can you explain that please?

Billy: Yeah, sure. You see, it was no accident that Haddie arrived when she did. I had learned when we first met that there was something cosmic in our relationship. There was something between us that was not of this world. It was just a feeling really, something I could not define or understand as a young man. I really began to understand it more just by watching and listening to Haddie. She was connected somehow to an energy much larger than either of us. I never attempted to define it but I simply watched Haddie and learned.

Anyway, Haddie later told me that on the day I had chosen to take my life, she had been sitting in her kitchen, sipping a cup of tea when the wind blew some napkins off the counter and her attention suddenly became focused on a mosaic tile on the wall. In the tile she saw an image of me preparing to take my life. Now, most people would have moved on from that thought and called themselves crazy, but not Haddie. She knew what was taking place. She didn't hesitate for a single moment. She jumped to her feet and raced right over here. The funny thing is, she didn't even know I was in town. But she didn't stop to think about it. You know the rest of the story. I honestly believe it was an angel who blew those napkins off the counter and presented the image to her. You might not believe it, but that's okay with me. I do.

G: That's quite a story. You honestly believe an angel intervened on your behalf?

Billy: Yes, I do. Had it been anyone else but Haddie, I might consider it false. But ever since I've known her, she has had this incredible way of knowing things. I asked her how she could do this and she told me we all could. It's just a matter of tuning in. Anyway, she told me it was an angel who had sent her and she did save my life, and I'm eternally grateful.

G: I can't argue with that. What happened during and after rehab?

Billy: Rehab was great. I mean, it stunk while I was there. It's pretty depressing to hit bottom like I did. Most folks there were just like me. They came from different places and circumstances, but their ultimate circumstance was the same. We all had a very big problem with substance abuse. Some of them fight it, though. A whole bunch of them didn't want to be there. They were placating loved ones or employers, whatever. But personally, I wanted to do it. I honestly did. Not for me, but for Haddie. And my dad. Motivation is the key to recovery. I was motivated. I understood I was being given a second chance, and I was determined not to screw it up. That's why I made it. There's no magic involved. It's hard work setting your mind up to think the right way, but it can be done.

I did the whole twelve-step program. It sounds like a strange indoctrination to those who don't experience substance abuse, but it's a very good road map for those who do. After I was released from rehab, I began attending meetings. It's a very awkward thing to do. You've all seen them on TV or in the movies. But I got past the initial discomfort by keeping the goal as my focus. It helped me understand that it was a means to an end. The end to which I'm referring is the ability to remain free from the demons and what they do to your life. When you see it that way it becomes easy, actually. Anyway, I've been sober ever since, and that's how it happened.

G: Sounds as if your story has a happy ending.

Billy: Sort of.

G: Sort of?

Billy: Yeah, for the most part it has been that way. There were a few more battles and circumstances to get past, but it turned out okay.

G: You've aroused my curiosity. Battles sound kind of serious.

Billy Smalls

Which would you like to describe first?

Billy: I suppose the first would be the matter of the money that was embezzled from me during my career. I'm not one to talk about specific figures, but it was quite a bit. Once again, Haddie saved me, at least her attorneys did. She had incredibly powerful connections. I don't have to describe to you what that means. When my former manager saw what he was dealing with, he settled up real fast. He knew he'd be in jail for a very long time; he was not a naive man. I did not recover my full estate. He couldn't produce the entire amount. But I did well enough to satisfy my lawyers and myself. I then invested my money with Haddie's people, and money has never again been an issue.
   That's the sum and total of that one.

G: It sounds pretty simple. I'm sure it's a bit more detailed than that, but I've learned you are a man of a few words. Thanks for sharing though. What else do you wish to talk about?

Billy: What happened between Haddie and me.

G: I was hoping that would be the one. I'm most curious to hear about your relationship.

Billy: Well, it's not your classic Hollywood love story, but like everything else about us, it's just different from the mainstream. See, after I had been through the rehab and active in the program, Haddie and I rekindled our affair. We became mad about each other, just like in the old days. It began one day after I had returned from a meeting. Haddie was in the apartment, cleaning and straightening things up. She did that a lot since William had died. Anyway, we hadn't made love in years. We loved each other through all the trials and tribulations, I knew that deep down inside. Yet we hadn't touched each other. But that evening when I returned, I could feel her desire the moment I walked through the door. I didn't even have to see her; I could actually feel it. When I did see her and looked into her eyes, I knew. I must have been looking at her the same way because we didn't even speak. We just exploded into each other's arms. It was so wild, so wonderful! It was like the old days, only better. Like so many other things about Haddie, I can't explain the why or how this happened. I've learned when it comes to her to just accept what takes place. But I can tell you this: in a single moment I realized just how much I loved her, how much I had missed her. She was my twelve-step program. She was my inspiration. She was my music, my most precious song.

We've been lovers since that moment. I suppose we'll be lovers for all of eternity.

I Wish You Love

Well I wish you peaceful dreams, as you go to sleep
And I ask the lord above, that your soul He'll keep
And I wish you sunshine playing in a sky of blue
There's a special wish I have I'm wishing just for you
I wish you love

Billy Smalls

Well I wish you rainbows after each and every rain
And a life of happiness that's free from tears and pain
I wish you peace and harmony in everything you do
And this special wish I have, I'll wish again for you
I wish you love

Heaven knows I just adore you,
I'll never place anyone before you
I wish you all the best in life
May the angels walk beside you,
may you feel a hand to guide you
And may your days be filled with sunny skies

May I be the very best friend that you'll ever know
May your heart carry me inside you everywhere you go
May I share your laughter and I'll take away your pain
And this special wish I have, I'll wish it once again
I wish you love…

G: I become amazed whenever you describe things about Haddie. She sounds so intriguing. Would you care to share anything more about your life with her? I understand and respect your attitude regarding privacy. However, I'm just very interested.

Billy: I do have some things to share. Normally I would keep these things to myself, but I've agreed to tell my story. There's some more to tell, so I will.

G: Thank you. Would you please tell me more about your relationship with Haddie?

Billy: Okay, here goes. Haddie and I were really enjoying our new relationship. We were living life a day at a time. I'd learned to do that through the program, and Haddie had learned to do that with the loss of William. His passing had a profound effect on us both.

G: You briefly mentioned his passing. How did that affect you both?

Billy: It was traumatic for Haddie. Her relationship with him was a beautiful one in reality. William was an incredibly powerful man from an incredibly powerful family. I've mentioned before he was well traveled and in his travel he tasted a variety of women. I don't know if he had other women to whom he professed love. Neither does Haddie. Not for sure anyway. However, he and Haddie did love each other in a different sort of way. They were true friends. They enjoyed each other's company. Haddie respected William very deeply, and he respected her in return. He did not respect women in general, but it was different when it came to Haddie. He discussed his business affairs with her and valued her opinion and advice. They did little things together. They went to dinner, the movies, shopping. All the things normal couples do. Of course the frequency of these things was not what normal couples experience. William was not home a whole lot. But when he was, they did very well together. The only place they didn't really connect was in bed. Haddie did not excite William. That's one I'll never understand. She's the most exciting woman I've ever tasted, and I've been around my share of women. I just didn't get what was in his mind. But to be truthful, I'm happy about that.

Anyway, you already know how Haddie and I came to be. I suppose we would have continued to live that way had William not become ill. But his illness changed it all.

When William was diagnosed with prostate cancer, Haddie was deeply concerned. She didn't want to lose him. It wasn't because of the wealth and status he had brought to her life. Haddie was not that way. She really cared. It was because of her caring and her ability to see into the future, that she decided to dedicate her entire self to William's final days on earth. Those final days took about nine years, but Haddie remained loyal to him each and every day. I had a difficult time with her dedication while it was taking place. I've told you about my anger and how it drove me wild. When I reflect on the entire scenario I suppose my immaturity created my cruelty. I was cruel to Haddie during those years. She needed my moral support, but I denied her what she needed. My interpretation during that time was that I was being rejected for another man, one who was not as good as me. Pretty selfish, huh? In retrospect, Haddie should have thrown me in the garbage, should have seen how shallow I was. But she didn't. Thank God she didn't. She understood my pain and what was motivating my actions. She understood and did not condemn me for the way I was behaving. I can't change the things I've done in the past but I certainly can control what I do in the present. There is not a circumstance on this earth or in the entire universe that will ever cause me to disrespect or hurt Haddie in any way. She has been my mentor since the day we met and will continue to be for all of eternity. I mention eternity because I've learned from her that we truly are eternal. I've also learned that Haddie and I will live this eternity together. We are more than soul mates, we are twin flames. We are two parts of the same soul. Our soul is linked forever and I'm awfully happy about that. I truly am.

G: That's a beautiful description. Very beautiful. Did you become inseparable and live happily ever after? Pardon the cliché, but I am getting the feeling there were still a few bumps in the road.

Billy: You're a very perceptive man. Yeah, we did have a few rough spots along the way.

See, Haddie and I became settled in, so to speak, for about three years after the death of William. We continued our relationship very privately. We had begun our relationship that way. It was important that no one know of our life together. Haddie had taught that to me early on. There was too much at stake to get caught. Well, we came to enjoy our own little world, and that's how we continued it. It's very exciting when you give it some thought. The fact that we had created our own secret world and had managed to maintain it was stimulating to us both. Others might not think that way, but once again it's okay with us. We just live our life as we see it and are secure in who we are. Anyway, that's how it progressed until Haddie wanted it to be different. I was shocked when she proposed marriage one day. We were sitting right in this recliner, all close and comfortable, when she came right out with it. I was shocked, I really was.

G: Did you accept her proposal?

Billy: No, I turned her down.

G: Why!

Billy: Because she had too much to lose and I had the road calling my name.

G: You'll have to explain this one. I'm so surprised by this!

Billy: Well, let me tell you, I was surprised by this also. But it made sense in the long run. See, Haddie was nearing fifty when this happened. She had given it a lot of thought. She realized that if she did marry me the truth of our relationship would be revealed somehow. She also knew that once she did, William's family would disinherit her. Her assets were sheltered in a trust that William had established for her while he was alive. The trustee of the fund was his brother, Alan. Alan had not been particularly kind to Haddie over the years. The problem stemmed from a time when he had come on to her and she rejected him. She had made an enemy. She had never told William of his brother's actions and William had not spoken to his brother about his coolness toward his wife over the years. He might have had his suspicions, but I suppose he didn't really want to know.

Haddie did receive funds from the trust as she requested them. Alan was resolved to honor his brother's request. However, she realized that once her infidelity became known, Alan would find ways to dissolve the trust and claim the assets for his own. His family possessed tremendous wealth and powerful connections. Haddie could not win, and she knew it. However, she still wanted to marry me.

I was extremely flattered by her proposal. Haddie and I had been together, on and off, for over eighteen years at that point. Try keeping a secret for that long. It seems impossible, but we managed to do it. However, I was no longer the wide-eyed teenager Haddie had met so long ago. I was now much older, probably older than my years in many ways. I had experienced so much by this time in my life. I had gone from bottom to top and back to bottom again. The bottom is not a very comfortable place. It's one I did not care to return to. It's somewhere that I did not want Haddie to experience. Even though at that point in my life I had enough assets for us to live well for a long time, I could never offer Haddie a certain security that I realized she was entitled to. That may seem to be a shallow perception. After all, true love conquers all, so they say. Yet it was through true love that I saw into the future. Haddie had taught me how to do this.

I have always harbored in my being a fear of life's ending. I understand that we go on living, in some form of existence. We are made of energy, and energy does not get destroyed. It might be transformed, but not destroyed. Anyway, my dad's passing had a very profound effect on me. The realization that we could slip off this planet at any time was difficult for me to deal with. I had also become aware of the infirmities of old age and the indignities that the world imposes on the senior population. People dwelling in their "golden years" do not always experience the fulfillment of their dreams. It all too often becomes a living nightmare and a time when death becomes an attractive alternative for so many. I had come to see that wealth plays a great role in the quality of care and comfort one is offered during those times. I knew Haddie and I had many quality years ahead of us. I was deeply and passionately in love with her. But I did not want her to forfeit what she had earned during her life with William. The fortune William had left was hers, and she deserved it. I did not want a penny of it. I would make my own way, but I wanted it for Haddie. I wanted to be certain that if life became an experience of frailty for her that she would have the best care possible. That's why I rejected her proposal. I'd do it again if she asked me.

G: That's very strong and very deep. How did Haddie handle it?

Billy: She didn't do well, at first. No one likes being rejected, even for the right reasons. I suppose it might have been something about her age and cycle of life that was motivating her thinking. Her perception was that it didn't matter what would happen twenty-five years from that point. Living on a daily basis was the important thing. I agonized at her disappointment and pain. I honestly did, but I held fast to my belief. It took awhile, but Haddie came to understand the logic of my thinking and eventually was grateful that I held the line. I guess she took a good look around her and saw the way things work. But I didn't want to disappoint her, so I married her myself.

G: Married her yourself? I don't understand.

Billy: I wrote a ceremony and performed it right here in this room. I declared my love and devotion to her and she did the same for me. Our witnesses were the spirits of the universe, and God. We didn't need a man dressed in a robe to let the universe know we declared ourselves to be man and wife. We knew, and God knew. That's all that mattered to us. We didn't exchange rings, we exchanged matching necklaces. And do you know what? Our union is as sacred to us as that of any man and woman on this planet. We are man and wife. Our vows and our union are sacred in our eyes, and that's all that counts. You might or might not agree. It's just the way it is.

G: I suppose I can't really dispute that point. It's a very unusual perception, and I'm sure you'd be tolerant of me if I didn't get it for a while. You and Haddie certainly have lived life quite differently from me and those I know. However, speaking with you certainly offers me a different view of living. You are a most interesting man. Now, a moment ago you said another reason for the "bumps in the road" regarding you and Haddie had to do with the road calling. Care to explain that one?

Billy: That's a fair question. I guess I went through a midlife crisis. I had been getting back into the music scene, as my recovery became a permanent way of life. I pretty much kept to studio work. I was doing a jingle thing on a regular basis. It was the safest way for me to keep my hand in the music and out of the world of the demons. I didn't want temptations thrown at me too soon, although I doubt I would have indulged. My years of oblivion and pain were etched powerfully into my being. Anyway, after a while something started to happen within me. I began writing new songs. They just came to me. Through me actually. It was as if I had turned on a faucet and the songs just poured right through. It was incredible. At first I sold them. It wasn't hard for me to find buyers. I still had a reputation in the business. It's a smaller world than you might imagine. Well, initially I was thrilled. A few heavy hitters were buying my songs and making them work.

It was a good feeling, but only at first. After a while I wanted to play and record my songs. I spoke with Haddie about it. We both knew that if I did this, a natural progression follows. If the labels like the work, then I'd wind up doing promotions and gigs. That involved traveling, lots of it. I was not crazy about it for a few reasons. First, it was hard. It could be exciting but not everyone realizes the time and stress that occurs when you involve yourself like that. Second, I would have to spend lots of time away from Haddie. Even though we were married in our own way, we were not married in the eyes of the world. Especially the McDowell world. It would be too difficult to mask our relationship if Haddie were to travel with me. There were strong reasons for me not to go.

G: But you did go. What motivated you to do it?

Billy: It was this feeling deep within my soul. It was stronger than logic. It just kept calling me, and I responded. I just had to go.

G: You did? What was it like being back out there?

Billy: It was actually great. I did have a difficult time at first. I was filled with apprehension about so many things. First of all, how would the fans receive me? Then there was the issue about parties and so forth. And of course Haddie.

Haddie had made it easy for me to go. I knew she was uneasy about this event in our lives, but she was unbelievable about it. She assured me that she would be fine. She would be safe and comfortable. That, by the way, was my greatest concern. She also made me feel that I was doing the right thing. She told me I had truly been offered some very special gifts from the universe by way of the music and it was actually my karmic responsibility to take it to the heights that it was destined to achieve. That was the key to my leaving. I knew she was correct about that.

Well, I did hit the road, and it was wonderful. I was determined to do my best and to absorb every ounce of positive energy I possibly could. It took a couple of months to feel settled and comfortable, but then it became so fine. The fans were receiving me very well. They all knew my story about battling the demons. America is a wonderful country. People here are very willing to forgive and forget; they embrace people who were down and out and then fight their way back to the top. My band also made things easy for me. I was traveling with a pretty seasoned group of musicians. They all had their

Billy Smalls

own issues and ways of life, but they were wise and considerate enough to leave me alone when it came to the partying. They did what they did but didn't force their good times on me. That was the easy part. The harder part was all the attention I was receiving from the women.

G: You had issues of fidelity along the way?

Billy: Yeah, unfortunately, I did. I did not intend it to be so, but it happened. You see, I was now a middle-aged man with quite an unusual history. I thought I would never miss the adulation of the rock star gig. I thought I was way past that line of thinking, but the truth is, I was not. I had gone from a celebrity to a nobody, a washed up substance abuser. I had lost my confidence and self-respect. Even though I had regained my sense of who I was, I guess somewhere down deep I still longed to be a star. But stardom requires a price. You have to be available to the fans if you want the limelight. And once you are there, so many things become available to you on a daily basis. Everyone wants a piece of the star. Everyone wants a story to tell at a party or at the office. Women become very aggressive toward you. Most of us think when we hook up with a woman, we are conquerors. The truth is many times we are the ones being conquered. They become distant memories to us but sometimes we become a notch in their belts. Think this through and you'll come to understand the truth of it.

Well, I did not indulge at first. I managed to avoid the temptations of drugs and alcohol. I did well avoiding all the sexual encounters that were taking place around me. I was holding fast to my love for Haddie and honoring our marriage.

But the time I spent with her was becoming less and less. I missed her, and I missed our physical contact. It was the trip to Europe that did me in. I was away from her for so long that I needed a taste of something physical. A very attractive young lady in London was the first mistake I made. There were a number of others that came after that. At first it was unsettling to me, but after a while it became easier to rationalize in my mind. But the truth is, I had encountered another demon in my life. This time it was sex. I did not recognize it at first, but that's what had happened. The demons were determined to claim my soul. I had allowed them to re-enter.

G: You slept with many different women? How did that affect your life with Haddie?

Billy: It ruined it, almost forever. Had it not been for my dad, I'm certain we could never have resolved this problem.

G: Your dad helped you? I need to have this explained to me.

Billy: Okay, but it will take a little while. See, when I returned from Europe, I suddenly became filled with guilt about my infidelities. I was so absorbed in guilt that I couldn't touch Haddie. I felt so dirty and remorseful for cheating on her. It was not very difficult for Haddie to figure out. We had a great physical life together, and suddenly I was not coming near her. She confronted me about it, and I decided the best thing to do was to come clean. I confessed my infidelities, all of them, in hopes she would understand and forgive me. I tried to convince her that they meant nothing to me—it was just a physical need that a man, any man, experiences. I figured she would understand that mindset. However, it did not turn out that way. She did not say a word to me. She just looked at me, actually right through me, then walked out the door. Not a word, not a tear, not a single emotion. She just walked out the door.

    Haddie was gone and I thought it would be forever.

Winds Of Change

I remember when it was you and me,
running wild and free
And I loved you each and every day
Always you and me,
that's all I can see all my live-long days
And I held you in so many ways
But the winds of change, when they start to blow
They can try to blind you, steal your very soul

So I went away, and I learned to play
All those cheating games
And I couldn't see how much I changed
I'd forget to phone, leave you all alone,
didn't pay you no mind
And I treated you so unkind, I was blind
But the winds of change, when they start to blow
They can try to steer you, show which way to go

So I changed my ways, didn't want to play
No more empty games,
and I thought you'd be there when I called
When I got back home, found myself alone,
you had gone away
And I realized the price I'd have to pay, every day
But the winds of change, when they start to blow
They can try to heal you, bring peace to your soul

Now I think of you, with a love so true
No more tears to cry, and I wish you all the best in life
Maybe winds will blow and they'll let you know
That I will be here if you ever want me by your side,
be my bride
Well the winds of change, when they start to blow
Maybe they can find you, bring you back home…

I became so lost, so alone. I became filled with contempt for the life I was living. I resolved at that moment to quit the music industry. I would never step into that scene again.

G: That's terrible! Please tell me what happened between you and Haddie!

Billy: Nothing. Not for a very long time. She wanted nothing to do with me. She had understood so many things about me over the years and had tolerated so much. But this was different. We had declared our allegiance to each other in the eyes of God and the universe, and I had violated our vows. They were sacred to Haddie, and she expected them to be sacred to me.

Billy Smalls

In My Heart I Can Hold You

Many nights I sit here just thinking,
about the love for you I feel inside
And how in my heart I can hold you
How I wish I could hold you in my arms

Well this love I feel, it's strong and mighty;
it's a love that you and I both know
Still it's in my heart I can hold you
How I wish I could hold you in my arms
Because I love you…with all my heart

Day and night my heart and soul remember
Special moments that you and I once shared
How I long for just one precious moment
So I could tell you just how much I care for you,
my every prayer is for you

And that, you will always be my one true lover;
you will always be my one true love
Still it's in my heart I can hold you
How I wish I could hold you in my arms
Because I love you…with all my heart

    Well, I became devastated, to say the least. Not only because of my loss of Haddie, but because of the loss I had inflicted on her. That was the worst of all. I knew how pain felt. It was one thing for me to experience it, but it was too much to bear knowing I had created it for Haddie. She was, and still is, the most wonderful being I have ever, or will ever encounter in my lifetime—in any lifetime, for that matter. I am so fortunate that she came to forgive me. That's where my dad comes in. It was his intercession that brought us back together. I say this each and every day, sometimes a hundred times: "Thank you, Dad. Thank you so very, very much!"

G: I'm a bit baffled at this moment. I'm learning that you are very different from most others. You've experienced things most of us cannot even fathom. I'm not sure I understand how your deceased father helped you and Haddie become reunited. But I am most eager to find out. You will elaborate, won't you?

Billy: Yes, gladly. I would like anyone reading this to understand how things truly work. It will be beneficial to anyone alive and will contribute to the good of the entire universe if we all come to grips with the reality and power of Spirit. Here's what happened.

I had tried to contact Haddie for quite a while, but she refused to respond. I eventually came to understand that our life together was not going to happen, at least not for a long time. But I became incredibly determined to right the wrong. Not so much for me, but for Haddie. I had created a deep pain in her soul, and I decided to dedicate my entire existence to alleviating her pain. I had no idea how this could be accomplished. The only thing I could think of was to pray.

I could not remain in this apartment any longer. Its history was overwhelming. I perceived that if I was to stay, I would eventually return to drug and alcohol abuse. That would

Billy Smalls

definitely have ended things; it would have been the nail in the coffin. I spent less and less time here. I checked into hotels and motels just to avoid being home. I began to attend churches of all denominations, trying desperately to find a way to bring Haddie back into my life. I had hit bottom once again, but it was worse this time. This time I was alone. However, it was not in the churches and temples that the solution appeared. It was in the window of Macy's at Herald Square that I found the answer to my prayers.

G: Okay, by now I'm ready to accept anything you have to say. I've given up attempting to infer how things take place in your life. You have to explain this one!

Billy: It's crazy, I agree. But that's where it happened.

I was wandering, rather aimlessly, around the city one afternoon. It was a gray day in December. The wind was chilling as it gusted down Broadway. I remember every detail of the day. Anyway, for some reason I stopped in front of Macy's and looked into the window. I was actually checking my reflection in the glass. I was staring at a very forlorn and ragged individual. I noticed the deep wrinkles that had formed in my forehead and the dark circles beneath my eyes. My hair was graying, and my stomach had become soft and paunchy. I was disgusted with the image that was confronting me. I was ready to move on because I could not bear to look at myself any longer.

But something suddenly caught my eye in the corner of the window display. In the upper left corner of the display was a small picture of a man and a young boy sitting on a dock. They each held a fishing pole in their hands. The man was looking peacefully toward the water. His back was toward me, and I could not see his face. But the boy was showing his profile. He was staring toward his father, looking up at his dad with admiration and love, seemingly asking with just a glance for his advice. I stared hard at the boy. I could not believe my eyes, for after a while I could swear that boy was the very image of me. I kept staring, then looking away and back again. I didn't want to delude myself into creating some illusion that would only increase my already deep depression. Yet each time I returned my gaze to that picture, it was the same. It was then that I realized that I was being offered divine intervention, and I understood at once what I had to do. It took a mere moment to comprehend what must be done.

G: Well, please tell me what had to be done!

Billy: I had to return home.

G: You had to go back to your apartment?

Billy: No, I had to return to my roots. I had to go back to Lindenhurst. I had to go back home.

G: Back home? That's very strange to hear you say that. You have not mentioned your family or hometown since you left for the city. Perhaps you will offer some insight into that now.

Billy: There isn't a whole lot to tell regarding my family. See, once I left I didn't return very often. The town brought back

Billy Smalls

too many painful memories. Most of my family had moved away, except for my brothers Tom and Jackie. My sisters were scattered around the Northeast, and mom had moved with my sister Lisa to Fairfield, Connecticut. She was doing well. I guess I was not the most attentive son when it came to mom. I did call her on a semi-regular basis over the years, but my visits were not as frequent as they should have been. To be honest I'm not entirely sure why. Perhaps I felt guilty for taking off on her and the family at such a young age. Perhaps I felt so poorly about my lifestyle that I just couldn't face her. Anyway, my brothers and sisters stuck it out and did eventually establish decent lives for themselves. However, that's something I really do not wish to discuss. I'm doing my best revealing my life to you, but there are some areas that I choose to keep to myself. My family is one of them. Don't be offended, but that's just the way it is.

G: No offense taken. I suppose we all have areas in our lives that we prefer to keep private. I respect your wish regarding your family. Now, from where would you like to continue?

Billy: From my old house. See, my brother Jack had remained in the old house on 29th Street. It hadn't changed much since we had lived there as kids. Jack didn't really modernize anything except to vinyl side the house. Same kitchen, same living space, same everything. Jack had remained pretty simple and reminded me of why I had left town. He had two kids and worked in the local bakery. He worked long hours, and his family was pretty much existing without his presence. He reminded me so much of my dad. He also reminded me that I had made the right move by leaving so many years ago.

Anyway, I was not sure how he and his family would handle things when I showed up at their front door on that Thursday evening in December. His wife and kids knew of me mostly through my music. I hadn't really interacted much with them over the years, and this made it very awkward when I suddenly appeared. Jack happened to be the one to answer the door, and we just stared at each other for a long time before I blurted that I was in deep trouble and needed to spend a few days in the old house. I was grateful that he made it easy for me and invited me right in. That single gesture fostered the energy that would eventually reunite my entire family. Once again, that's a story in itself, but not one I am here to discuss. My final reference to my family is that we have grown into a very cohesive unit, and all the pains and misunderstandings of the past have been resolved. Perhaps my father arranged that too. Nothing surprises me in the world of Spirit.

Anyway, the very next day I was down at the docks and staring out at the Great South Bay. I was surprised that it had changed so little over the years. The sights and sounds aroused so many memories within me. Although the December wind was biting at me, I managed to ignore its discomfort. The warmth of the memories was heating my soul. I was elated to discover that the "special place," as my dad used to call it, still existed. It was a small peer that jutted out about thirty feet into the water. Its planks were gray and weathered, and a few were broken and warped, but it still seemed the same. I walked out to the end and sat on its edge. My feet dangled above the water, just the way they used to. I closed my eyes and thought of my dad. The tears that streamed from my eyes managed to defy the attempt of the cold air to freeze them. They rolled effortlessly down my cheeks. I pushed all active thoughts from my head and listened to the sounds of the bay. I became lost in the rhythm of the water gently lapping the shore, the wind rustling the reeds, the gulls' shrill cry as they circled above. It was in the silence that dad came to me. It was in the silence that he told me the incredible news.

G: Your dad actually spoke to you? What was that like?

Billy: It is something difficult to describe in words. I mean, I didn't hear him externally. His voice didn't boom through the wind. It was inside that I heard him. I held my eyes shut, and I actually felt him sitting next to me, looking out at the bay as he used to do every time he had something important to say. You might think my mind was deceiving me, convincing me of his presence, and that's okay if you do. But I know he was really there. I need not explain that to anyone. I simply knew.

G: What did your dad tell you?

Billy: He told me how to bring Haddie back into my life. He told me to write to her and explain that Hannah had told her to return to my life. He told me write, and I quote, "In all of eternity there is but one mate for our soul. The one who completes us exists at all times. When the link appears, it must be bound to the chain. One must ignore the pain and tighten the link; no matter how much effort it requires. Secure the link, and all will be well. *Soo-nah-mahnte, soo-nah-mhey.*"

G: What did that mean?

Billy: At the time I did not know. But I did exactly as my dad told me to do. He had never given me ill advice before, and I knew that what he was telling me would bring Haddie back. I simply knew.

G: Are you telling me that Haddie returned after you sent that message?

Billy: Yes, she did.

G: Wow! This is a bit cosmic for me. However, I've learned to believe you, no matter how strange it may seem. By the way, who was Hannah?

Billy: Hannah was Haddie's grandmother. The words that I had written were her final words to Haddie. Hannah had spoken to my father and told him what I must say.

G: Her deceased grandmother spoke to your deceased father, who in turn spoke to you! I am deeply intrigued by this affair. Of course I am a bit skeptical.

Billy: That's okay if you feel that way. I probably would too if someone was telling this to me. But it's the way it happened.

G: I believe you; it's just strange to hear of such things. I would like to hear a bit about Hannah, if you don't mind discussing her. You had mentioned that Haddie was adopted. Was Hannah her biological grandmother, or was she her grandmother through adoption?

Billy: Hannah was her biological grandmother. If you recall I had mentioned that Haddie was in her forties when she discovered her roots. For a specific reason, her adoptive parents never told her the truth about her situation. Haddie never knew she was adopted. Her parents took this secret to their respective graves. Haddie probably would have never known about this had it not been for what you might call a chance meeting in the park. By now you'll come to understand that it was not really a matter of chance, not when it comes to Haddie. Anyway, it was on a stroll in Central Park that the truth was revealed.

G: This sounds awfully good. Is it there she met Hannah?

Billy: No, it was there that she met her mother. Here's what happened.

Haddie had gone for a walk in the park one Sunday afternoon in May, which was her routine at that time. She loved to walk alone in the park. Anyway, as she approached the skating rink, she noticed an elderly woman sitting alone on of the benches surrounding the rink. Haddie felt a strong inclination to go over to the woman and say hello. There was something about the woman's posture that projected loneliness, and Haddie felt a compulsion to ease the woman's seemingly troubled spirit. She approached the woman and asked if she would mind some company. The woman glanced toward Haddie, and her eyes nearly bulged from her head. An expression of shock captured her face, and her limbs became stiff. Haddie was concerned that the woman was having a stroke and placed her hands on the woman's shoulder and asked if she needed help. The woman could not remove the shocked expression from her face, and her body began to tremble. Haddie was ready to run and call for help. As she turned to head for help, the woman's hand suddenly clutched her jacket. She whispered, "Please don't go. You've been gone so long." Haddie gave her a puzzled look. The woman then said, "You are my daughter." Well, you can imagine the confusion that ensued from that point. It's a very long story but I'll attempt to tell it in a nutshell.

I've mentioned before that Haddie was the illegitimate child of a wealthy politician and a gypsy mother, Rabka. Her paternal father's career would have been ruined had the truth of this child been discovered. He was a married man, perceived by the public as a fine and upstanding family man. He was a high ranking and ambitious member of the New York political machine. His career eventually advanced into the United States Senate. Haddie had come to know him as a wonderful senator, but never as her father. She prefers to this day to keep his identity anonymous.

Her father was not a callous and uncaring man. Haddie has come to learn that he deeply loved her mother. He would sneak away often to meet her in very discreet places. Rabka loved him in return. However, she knew their relationship would never be more than the beautiful rendezvous they shared. Neither intended to conceive a child, and Haddie's birth caused their relationship to diminish. Although their relationship as lovers had to be diminished, her father made provisions to take care of the child. He wanted what he considered the best for her, thus the arrangements were made for adoption. Rabka was opposed to his plan but eventually relinquished her objections when she came to think in terms of her daughter's future. With great reluctance she agreed to have the child adopted upon her birth. Rabka held Haddie for just a brief moment before she bade her goodbye. Yet in that single moment, her daughter's face became etched in her memory. Her daughter would live forever in her soul.

G: That's quite an unbelievable story. You said Haddie knew her father as a senator. Would you explain that please?

Billy: Well, the senator arranged the adoption. He knew Haddie's adoptive parents quite well. They had been significant contributors to his early campaigns and had become close friends over the years. They were childless, and he had a child. Very simple. The arrangement was made with the promise that Haddie would know nothing of her adoption. The senator could not risk a scandal. As I mentioned, in those days it would certainly have ended his career. Scandals and infidelities were not revealed to the public as they are these days. There was no room for mistakes back then. Having Haddie being reared by his friends gave him access to her, in a bizarre kind of way. However, he loved her deeply in his own way, and did the best he could under the circumstances to support her. He gave generous gifts for all the appropriate occasions. He attended family celebrations. Haddie came to regard him as a kind of uncle. I realize this is most difficult to understand, but the world of wealth and politics is a world of its own. The rules that exist there are not the same rules that exist in the general society. Haddie would never have known the truth had she not met her mother.

G: I get the feeling you do not wish to discuss this issue much further. We are getting sidetracked regarding the reunion of you and Haddie. However, I do have a few questions pertaining to this segment of Haddie's life. One is, how did her natural father treat Rabka after Haddie had been adopted? Also, what happened in the relationship between Haddie and Rabka once the truth was revealed? Lastly, how does Hannah factor into the equation?

Billy: They're all fair questions, and I'll address each one briefly.

The first question you asked pertained to the relationship of the senator and Rabka. I mentioned that he loved her deeply. He carried this love to his grave. He always made sure Rabka was provided for financially, and he helped her to live comfortably. Rabka loved him in return. It was difficult for her to have abandoned her baby, but she felt she did the proper thing in the long run. She did not want her child referred to as a bastard and realized how difficult the child's life would be. Rabka understood that her daughter was being offered the opportunity to live a privileged life, a life she could not offer her daughter. She realized that her child would be cared for in a genuine and loving way. It was in the best interest of her daughter that she consented to the adoption. She did harbor an inner resentment for the senator along those lines, but she was savvy enough to understand that it was in their daughter's best interest for the severance to take place. It's an odd love story, but a love story just the same. I suppose just about everything about this interview defies convention, but the truth is being told.

Your second question was about Haddie and Rabka. To tell you the truth—I have not witnessed so much joy in all my life. It turns out that Rabka is just as special as Haddie regarding the things they see and understand. They amaze me, totally. I've learned so much by being in their presence. So very much. Perhaps the most significant lesson I've learned from watching them is that life is always now. Life is meant to be lived in the present moment. The past doesn't matter—it's just something that's happened. Too many of us are hung up on the past. We dwell on our mistakes, wrongs committed against us, wrong we've committed against others. We have no power to change the past. Our true power lies in how we live in our present. This present will in turn shape our future. Haddie and Rabka have taught me that every moment is precious and should not be lived in vain. They simply blow me away. Anyway, Haddie and Rabka are still very closely knit. Rabka is quite elderly now but still vital. Perhaps she might choose to speak with you at some time. It would be a most interesting experience to hear what she has to say. I've come to love her in a very special way. I'm sure you would too, given the opportunity.

Finally, about Hannah. Hannah was the true matriarch of the family. She immigrated from Romania, filled with the traditions of her culture. She was well aware of her daughter's relationship with her lover and did not approve of the affair. However, she never intervened because she had a vision of the future and understood that a karmic event was taking place. It was not in her power to interfere in this matter. Her abilities

The Spirit's Self-Help Book

empowered her to "see" the eventual reunion of mother and daughter. I suppose she also had the foresight to understand that Haddie and I were destined to reunite and spend the autumn of our lives devoted to each other. That's why she said those words to Haddie not long before she passed on. Haddie did not really comprehend the meaning when Hannah spoke them, but when I wrote those words to her, she completely understood. That's why she did not hesitate to find me as soon as she read my letter. It was Hannah who brought her back to me. I did not meet her, but I love her with all my heart. I'm very fortunate to be included in such an incredible family of spirits.

G: Spirits?

Billy: Yes, spirits. We're all spirits, you know. I could spend a whole lot of time discussing this with you but I'll save that for another time. But yes, Haddie and her family are truly spirits. At some time in each individual's existence, he or she will come to understand this concept. It's for real.

G: Coming from you, I don't doubt it. Please clarify one more point before moving on. When you described Hannah's final words to Haddie, they concluded with, *"Soo-nah-mahnte, soo-nah-mhey."* These words intrigue me. Would you please tell me what they mean?

Billy: I would if I could, but I can't. I've asked Haddie what they meant so many times, but she just won't tell me. She said that one day the meaning will be revealed and that's all there is.

Perhaps I'm not meant to know. Perhaps you, or some reader, are destined to understand.

G: You're a very different man, Billy. This is an incredible experience interviewing you.

Billy: I am who I am, that's all.

G: That's quite obvious. Now, let's get back to you and Haddie. Please tell me about your lives once you reunited.

Billy: Our life together has been so fine ever since. I expect it will be until the day we pass to another dimension.

G: Haddie returned right away and all was well? Forgive me for saying this, but that sounds a bit contrived.

Billy: You're forgiven. I don't judge anyone. But that's what did happen. See Haddie knew that the message was from Hannah. That's why she was so quick to forgive. I'm not sure she'll ever forget, but she did forgive me. Haddie understands the universe and how it works. She was not about to waste her existence in lament and bitterness once she received the message. She understood her grandmother was informing her that it was time to enjoy the completion of her soul. We may go numerous lifetimes without that taking place. It's a difficult concept to grasp, but it's the truth. Anyway, you know by now I don't enjoy making stories very long, so let it go that Haddie and I patched up our differences and have been enjoying ourselves ever since.

Gypsy Girl

Gypsy girl, pretty girl, my whole world
Is centered in your love
Magic eyes, oh so wise, hypnotize me
With your precious love

Only you know the magic way to move me
Only you can thrill me in the night
When we meet and we put our souls together
I feel peace and all my world is right

Gypsy girl, pretty girl,
my whole world is centered in your love
In this world, just one girl, moves my soul,
so very deep inside

I'm the man with the magic way to move you
I'm the man who thrills you in the night
When I put my loving arms around you
I feel your peace and I know your world is right
Oh you are my love

Only I can know you as the gypsy;
only I can know you deep inside
I am just so captured by your beauty
And in your heart I always will confide my love

Billy Smalls

Gypsy girl, pretty girl,
my whole world is centered in your love
Take my hand, understand,
that my love is till the end of time

I will love you always and forever;
I will journey always by your side
I will love you truly and completely;
I will love you till the end of time
Oh you're my love…

G: Has your life changed since you've become reunited?

Billy: Yes it has, big time.

G: Would you be kind enough to explain?

Billy: Sure, I've gone this far. I won't leave you hanging.
    I did go through a number of changes. The first was regarding my fidelity. Ever since that day I lost Haddie, I have not been with another woman in any way. By *any way* I mean even in my mind. That includes memories as well as fantasies. That's a tough one for any man, or woman for that matter. But I made a vow to Haddie that I would conduct myself that way and have remained true to that vow since the moment I made it. I think conquering drug and alcohol addiction has helped me understand I can conquer anything. I've learned that life is totally in each individual's mind. We can't control external circumstances, but we can control how we react to them. That's a lesson that's etched more than in my mind—

it's etched indelibly into my soul. I'll carry that to whatever dimensions I travel from here.

Another change was my retirement from the music business, this time for good. I just could not handle the scene any more. It was the vehicle for the demons to attack me, and they hit me hard over the years. Of course I'm grateful for all the business has given me. I say prayers of thanks every day. I'm financially secure because of the time I spent there, and I have some very good friends that I truly love. I've been part of some incredibly creative energy. I'm also so much stronger because of all I've been through. However, I'm finding age is mellowing me a bit, and I no longer wish to face those kinds of challenges. I've had to battle my ego to get to the place I'm at now, but I've done it. Of course I still do my share of playing. I could not exist without my music. I occasionally perform in small bars, parties, and picnics, things like that. But that's good enough for me. Now that life is simple, I'm actually enjoying it.

G: I suppose Haddie is happy with the way your life is progressing.

Billy: Yes, she is. There is a sadness taking place though.

G: Sadness? I don't understand.

Billy: This is something I will not elaborate on because it's personal to Haddie and me. She asked that I not reveal the details when I told her I was doing this interview. However, Haddie is experiencing some physical difficulties that require very intensive care and attention. We're not sure what it going to happen at this point, and I'm deeply concerned. It makes me love her even more deeply, for I now understand why she was so devoted to William during his difficult times. To be quite honest, I do believe in the power of prayer, and if you or any readers would care to include Haddie in your prayers, I would be most appreciative. I just know it would help. She's the most incredible spirit I have ever, or will ever know in my eternity. I wish with all my heart and soul to exist with her for a while longer in this dimension.

G: I'm very sorry to hear about Haddie, and I promise to remember her in my prayers.

Billy: Thank you.

G: Well Billy, I'm sensing that you've told me about all you wish to, and I must say I've enjoyed your story, I truly have. I'll ask no more questions about your life. I'm very grateful for all you've revealed to me, and I certainly hope all goes well for Haddie. Somehow I know it will. Now, each spirit that manifests his or her story through me has agreed to make a statement regarding the existence of spirit in the universe. In closing, would you please relate to us what you have to tell?

Billy: It's my pleasure to do so. There are a few things I have to say. The first is that spirits do exist in so many dimensions. You and all humans are spirits, just as I and others of my dimension are. What separates us is the frequency at which we vibrate. We can all learn to communicate with one another other by sensitizing ourselves to each other's frequencies.

Think of transmissions along airwaves and you will be able to understand my statement. There are so many simultaneous broadcasts filling your atmosphere, many of which you are not even aware. You tune a band on your radio or television and suddenly discover something "new" and find out it's been there all along. Discovering spirits of different dimensions works in a similar way. It's merely a matter of "tuning in," so to speak.

The second truth I wish to reveal is that we truly are eternal beings, each and every one of us. There are so many different states in which we can exist. Human incarnation is not the exclusive existence of a soul. We are all composed of energy, which cannot be destroyed. What happens often is that our form of energy is transformed and aligned with a different frequency. It is then that we exist in a different dimension. We are constantly guided toward existing at finer vibrations. However, all spirits possess free will at all times and, although guided, it is our choice as to how we respond. That's why so many humans decide to live life again and again on earth. Yet there comes a time in all of eternity when a soul will develop a finer vibration and move on. It's the natural process of the universe. One can spend thousands of years in various human incarnations before moving on. However, thousands of years measured by earth standards is merely a blink of the eye in the realm of eternity.

The final truth I wish to reveal is that each moment of existence should be savored. The human condition is a very difficult experience. Life on earth is filled with trials and tribulations. There are so many external circumstances imposed on a human that it often becomes an overwhelming existence. However,

Billy Smalls

the purpose of these trials is to alert the soul to the availability of the higher power. Humans are constantly being encouraged to attend to spiritual matters amidst the turmoil of daily life. Each moment is a lesson in free will. It might take centuries to master the concept, but eventually all human souls will. It is then that they will move on. My final statement is treasure life, treasure the higher power, and treasure your soul.

G: Those statements are quite profound, and I will remember them always.
   Thank you, Billy. You have been a most gracious and interesting spirit to work with. I promise to remember you always. Peace, my friend.

Billy: Peace to you and yours. Goodbye, G.

G: Goodbye, Billy. *Soo-nah-mahnte, soo-nah-mhey.*

Billy Loves Haddie

When I think of you I can't help smiling
Every thought of you is a thought of love
My heart beats true for you, there's no denying
And I'm always thanking God above

My heart's just got this simple way of knowing
That you'll always be my very best friend
I do recall the day of love's beginning
But I know this love will never end

The Spirit's Self-Help Book

And so I offer you this little love song
I'm hoping that you hear it in your soul
Well it's a song I plan to keep on singing
'Cause my love for you just can't grow old
No my love for you just can't grow old
Yeah, yeah, yeah…yeah…

The Chief
Life as an Individual Journey

Revealing the truth about The Chief is a daring enterprise on my part. He is someone so real to me that one might think of me as a bit deluded once our conversation comes to light. However, I'm hopeful that your meeting The Chief will allow you to consider that the world of spirit truly does exist and that human beings are a significant part of the spiritual realm. I was reluctant to print our dialogue, for it has been very personal to me over the past few years. I've spoken to The Chief quite extensively regarding my feelings, but he has persisted in his desire to conduct this interview. It is with complete deference that I have chosen to honor his request.

I don't recall the exact moment when The Chief entered my consciousness, but I do recall quite vividly where and why he manifested himself to me. I was having difficulty a few years ago regarding my relationship with a particular individual. He was someone quite offensive to my son and me, and my basic instinct was to confront him in a violent fashion. Knowing that it is much more difficult to suppress violence than to act upon it, I sought a prayerful route to help me overcome the adrenaline that was driving me crazy. The offense committed against us was not a physical assault; it was an assault on our egos and a matter of control.

The details are not significant, but what is important to reveal is that the human ego is largely responsible for the inhumanity of our race. It often takes no more than a few words or a hand gesture to spark violence among us. Words spoken in anger can result in the breaking of family ties, can dissolve wonderful friendships, can precipitate the involvement of masses of people to react with hatred toward those not known to them personally. I could go on and on describing situations where the ego has wreaked havoc on our planet but I will not, for I'm sure you are comprehending its power.

Understanding the necessity to overcome my violent instinct, I removed myself to a place I call my "sacred spot." It is a small area in a wooded portion of my yard that I have designated as a place of refuge. I had established a rule for myself upon the creation of this spot. The rule is that when I enter this area, I will permit no negative thoughts to dwell in my consciousness. I established this rule through an awareness of the universe's need to receive thoughts of *Light*, for I believe that energy is transmitted through the waves of our minds. It took a bit of conditioning before I mastered my mind, but in time I learned how to remove all negative thought from remaining there. Love is easy when it is reciprocal and convenient, but very difficult when our psyche has been offended. There have been many masters who have explained this concept throughout the course of humanity, and I'm quite grateful to those who have revealed this truth.

The Chief

    However, this is neither the time nor place to expound on personal philosophy, for it is time to meet The Chief. Needless to say it was during this time of reflection that The Chief entered my consciousness and did much to help me understand the true meaning of spirit and love. We have spent much time together since then, although we had become estranged for a while. However, he has returned to my consciousness and wishes to be revealed to you. I'm sure it is his wish to impart his spiritual wisdom in the hope that the universe will be strengthened and your spirit enlightened. It is my sincere pleasure to introduce him to you.

* * *

The Spirit's Self-Help Book

G: Hello, Chief, it is a pleasure and honor to be communicating with you.

Chief: *Shee-ha-ho-na, shee-ho-nee.* Greetings. It is my pleasure.

G: You certainly have made it clear that you wish to be included in this work. I'm extremely happy that you have chosen to communicate your insights to us. You are a very special spirit to me, and I'm sure that the readers will recognize your enlightened consciousness.

Chief: Thank you for the kind words, my young friend. I am simply who I am, as you and all souls are who you are. We are all unique and quite special. We are all part of the Creator; no matter what dimension in which we dwell. Although the universe is vast and gives life to so many, we are all part of the same universal energy. We are true brothers and sisters of spirit and soul. If all souls would allow themselves to understand this concept, then the universe would become more peaceful.

G: I understand the concept and find it a wonderful thought, but do you think that can really happen?

Chief: All is possible, though not probable. Souls possess a dual nature, and it is this duality that prevents the universe from becoming a place of pure *Light*.

G: I've always supposed that duality was something limited to human beings. I am learning from my communications with members of the spirit community that duality is present in many dimensions. Am I correct in this assumption?

Chief: Yes, you are correct and have become most perceptive. Your insight pleases me for you are becoming enlightened to the ways of spirit, which only strengthens the universe. However, the duality of which you speak manifests itself differently in each realm of the spirit world. The dimension in which it vibrates dictates the struggles of a soul. There is a great deal to discuss regarding this matter, but I am here to discuss the human condition with you and your kind. There exists a commonality in all souls, yet the trials of each dimension are unique. The human condition is difficult, for the soul's cloak is quite dense. The cloak to which I refer is the human body and the human mind.

G: I have many notions regarding this subject. I am eager to hear your insight. Please continue.

Chief: You must listen carefully to my words. What I am about to reveal is no secret; yet it must be read and comprehended through the soul, not the rational mind. The rational mind of "Humankind" is part of his problem. I will explain.

Man, as do all souls, possesses the inherent duality of good and evil. *Light* and *Darkness* are more appropriate spiritual terms. The *Light* within man knows of the existence of the higher power—the Creator exists in each and every human being. The more one aligns with this energy, the finer the vibration becomes. However, the earth is not designed to accommodate the perfect vibration of *Light*. There are many trials a soul must experience before it knows of the beauty and power of the *Light*. The basic instinct of man is survival. One's physical and emotional environment often makes enlightenment a low priority, for physical needs dominate one's consciousness. This is life at its most basic level, and many exist in this state. The trials for those in this position are the greatest on your planet. Although it appears as a cruel concept, it is in reality a tremendous opportunity for a soul to move toward the *Light*. The soul that recognizes the power of faith is the soul that grows in enlightenment.

G: Forgive me for interrupting, Chief, but I have a problem with that. I mean no disrespect by stating this, but it seems to me that so many people who are living an unfortunate existence spend an awful lot of time in prayer and merely accept their lot in life. It's as if they've created a fantasy world and are awaiting the Savior to descend from the sky and make life wonderful. They are waiting for the next life to come and are missing out on the life they are living. They are wasting precious moments in time.

Chief: That is a very perceptive observation and one I will now address. My compliments to you.

Enlightenment is often mistaken for inaction and blind acceptance of one's station in life. This perception has been created and fostered by those in positions of power. This mindset has been perpetuated by members of the ruling class which, by the way, includes the clergy as well as kings, presidents, nobles, and captains of industry. The concept of blind acceptance is a design to keep power in the hands of the few. Belief in a better world makes a miserable existence more tolerable, but also fosters inaction and maintains a safe and secure status quo for those who have learned to master the material ways of the planet. Of course there are always souls who gather to create a rebellion and are often successful in shifting the balance of power. Their intentions may be noble and just, but the common scenario is that once a new regime is created, then they become the "haves," so to speak, and tend to concentrate their efforts on reinforcing their new station in life. The lust for power is a danger to the soul, yet is a very basic instinct in man.

Enlightened souls recognize this and do not remain inactive. Enlightened souls move to free themselves of whatever conditions create misery to their human psyches. Those who become enlightened recognize the wholeness of the universe and the power of its being, not just the power of the material world. Human beings must learn to recognize the importance of creating *Light* and calling on that same *Light* to keep it free. It is freedom that alters the vibration of a soul to a finer frequency. It is freedom that fortifies the soul.

G: How does a soul become free?

Chief: The first thing souls must do is overcome physical desire. The physical desire to which I'm referring includes sexual lusts as well as lusts for power, drugs, alcohol, tobacco, and material possessions. The souls that constantly long for these things are bound by desire and are not free to enjoy the enlightened state of mind that is available to every human being on the earth. The active minds of those filled with lust create a constant distraction toward attaining a finer frequency of vibration of the soul. I am not stating that they should surrender all the joys that are a part of the human condition. It is not terrible to enjoy comfort and passion, for they do add strength to the spirit. However, what I am conveying is that addiction and obsession to the pleasures of the earth will only delay souls' enlightenment and ability to vibrate at a finer frequency. When this occurs, then less *Light* is generated into the universe and the opportunity for creating universal harmony is delayed.

G: Chief, are you suggesting that we surrender all our desires to the world of spirit? That almost sounds like the dogmatic principles that were imposed upon me as a child.

Chief: No, my friend. You have missed my point. The pleasures available to those in life exist for them to enjoy. However, how much enjoyment do they truly bring if people are constantly thinking only of these pleasures? What I'm referring to is the state of mind where they become obsessed by attaining these pleasures. When they do become obsessive, then these pleasures are usually not enjoyed, for the constant longing for more distracts the human psyche to the point of blindness. Money, sex, power are no longer satisfying, for the obsessed mind is never rested, never complete. The joy of the moment is missed, for, as the moment occurs, the mind is often thinking of how to attain more of its indulgence. If you take a moment to consider this statement, you will find that I am revealing a truth.

The Chief

G: How exactly is someone supposed to enjoy life's pleasures?

Chief: By detachment.

G: Detachment?

Chief: Yes, detachment. If souls learn to rise above the desire for carnal pleasure, then desire will be incapable of holding them captive. It's a very simple concept if you take time to consider its validity. Souls detach themselves by viewing an obsession as separate from the self. An obsession is not truly who you are; it is something that has attached itself to the soul. Many addictions are formed in the mind and are easier to expel, while others are a part of a soul's body chemistry and more difficult to control. However, the proper way to move beyond obsession is to recognize it as a debilitating force of energy and to move toward detachment. I am not suggesting that this is an easy task. Yet it is a necessary course for a soul's development. All souls will eventually seek enlightenment. Many souls are content to persist in battling the demons of obsession because, for them, the consequences do not outweigh isolated moments of pleasure. That is why souls do enter the realm of human existence many times. However, there will arrive a moment in a soul's journey when it will understand the power and beauty of *Light* and its ability to dwell in this precious energy. It is then that it will seek to detach itself from its obsessions and surrender to the force that is waiting to help it to shape its destiny. You should understand this truth, for there are many who are communicating with you at the present moment in your human existence.

G: I do understand that on a personal level, Chief. I am grateful for all who are coming forward and speaking both to and through me at this moment in time. I'm hopeful that those who read this book will glean some insights that assist them along their journey of life.

I have another question that I would like to ask of you. I understand the concept of obsession and how it is important to detach oneself. However, I often wonder about the plight of those who are born into poverty, captivity, war, and infirmity. How are these souls supposed to detach themselves from their severe conditions in life? Aren't these the souls that create a world of fantasy in their attempt to deal with the deplorable, debilitating, and often brutal conditions that life has imposed upon them?

Chief: These human beings do not create a world of fantasy. They exist on the same planet as you, but their reality is quite different. They have choices to make, as do you. However, the choices they have to make are different in many ways from those that souls devoid of such suffering must make. You must consider this statement. Some souls who exist in a state of agony are there because they have chosen to be, while others are there because of random circumstances.

G: Hold on, Chief, you've lost me with that one! I've often heard the concept that God gives each of us what we can handle in life. I'm not sure I believe that because I know a number of people whose lives are filled with constant suffering, either for themselves or their loved ones. It's difficult for me to rationalize that God has delivered these circumstances, but I do consider the possibility. It might be a form of rationalization, or it might be the truth. However, I've not really heard the alternative explanation of random circumstances. Please explain this to me.

Chief: Of course I will. There are billions of people on the planet earth, and each person is a soul. Each has its own individual energy, its individual perception of life. The bottom line is that all souls do seek enlightenment at some point in their existence. When this occurs, then life no longer becomes random. When a soul gives itself to the higher powers of the universe, then guidance is free to deliver itself to the searching soul. That is when the Creator will give the soul problems to solve, with the knowledge that the problems given are an opportunity to achieve strength and enlightenment. That is a simple and rational explanation.

However, not all souls of the planet are seeking enlightenment. Many have chosen to reject the concept of spiritual energy and purpose, and have consciously rejected the guidance available to them at any given moment. It is these souls that live life randomly. Some live quite well, some moderately, others an unfortunate existence. By removing themselves from the stream of spiritual consciousness, then they place their lives in a disordered existence. What happens to them is neither reward nor punishment; it is just a series of random circumstances. These are the souls that will surely reincarnate to the planet, perhaps many times. However, there will come a time in their existence when their soul will understand the concept of enlightenment and will seek its guidance. Your planet is a very interesting place for those of us who exist separately from it. There is so much energy emanating into the universe that is scattered and discordant. Should all souls reach the point of a consciousness that allows them to perceive the connection of all life, the awareness that all beings of the universe are capable of contributing to the *Light,* that a brotherhood of souls exists for the highest good of all creation, then harmony would reign in the universe. The beings of earth possess a tremendous power in the universe, but not all beings recognize this power. The truth is that the potential for harmony exists. That is why it is vital that those who understand spirit bear the responsibility of living their lives devoid of randomness and listen closely to the guiding forces that are available.

G: Thanks for the explanation. It has helped me to clarify an issue that has confused me for some time. I have another question. You mentioned that guidance is available, at any moment, to the soul who seeks it. Would you please elaborate on this concept?

Chief: Your curiosity is very healthy. I will explain. Consider this simple story. Two students are attending a major university. Both students possess an equal intellect and work ethic. The students encounter a course of study that is difficult for them to understand. One student struggles to achieve a passing grade but does not seek the help of the professor or the study teams available through the university. This student tries hard to achieve on his own, but his individual efforts are not good

The Chief

enough and he fails the course. The second student faces the same difficulty but decides to seek the professor and study team for assistance. As a result of their guidance, the course material becomes clear and this student passes with a respectable grade. That is how the world of spirit works for all who seek it. Guidance is available at all times, but it does not seek you. You must seek the guidance. How this guidance will manifest itself is different for each and every soul. However, when a soul learns to seek the guidance of spirit, then it will recognize the existence of spirit quite readily. It's a matter of attuning one's senses to the vibration of spirit. It is not a difficult or mystical process. Just seek however your spirit tells you, and you will find what you are looking for. The difficulty for most souls is recognizing the simplicity of spirit's manifestation and believing it to be true. The process of rational thought that has been fostered by your society often impedes the recognition of spirit. The average mind of your society needs to see concretely to believe.

G: I know this to be true. Why do you suppose it is so?

Chief: It exists this way for a few reasons. One is organized religion. The concept of religion is beautiful in and of itself. People who gather for religious reasons are generally sincere in their quest for a way to connect with spirit. This is a healthy practice, and it does generate light into the universe. The problem, however, is when practitioners practice their dogma and rituals with a blind faith. When practitioners of religion merely follows the leader of their religion, then they are often misguided and miss the true connection to spirit. The clergy bears a great responsibility. Members of the congregations look to them for guidance, and the souls are in the their hands.

However, many leaders of organized religion become filled with the power they have acquired and recognize that the means to maintaining and increasing this power is to impose controls over their congregation. They often become "spokesmen" for the Lord and remind their followers of the harsh realities of the Kingdom of God. By instilling fear into their followers's minds through the guise of their close relationship to God, these leaders exercise their power. It is a dangerous situation for those who follow blindly with the faith that their leaders will guide them toward nirvana. Dogma becomes established, and it is often this dogma that will separate people from one another. Judgments are formed against anyone who fails to believe in the dogma of one's faith.

I realize this sounds harsh, but look toward the history of your planet, and examine the wars and atrocities committed against members of your race which have been perpetrated through religious conviction. It becomes frightening when this takes place. The very spirit of God is violated in His name. Inhumanity, hostility, and condescending attitudes are often rooted in dogma. The belief that there is only one true way to worship is very often the attitude of many organized religions. Consider this thought, and you will understand its truth.

G: I certainly can agree with this perception, Chief. However, how does this impede one's recognition of spirit?

The Chief

Chief: Quite simply. When one becomes blinded by faith then he is no longer open to the subtle energies of spirit. The soul who has become captured by the rhetoric of empowered leaders looks only for what they are instructed to see. They develop a sense that there is only one way to communicate with spirit, which is whatever way they have been instructed to believe.

Spirit is not singular. It is vast and multi-faceted. Each soul has its own vibration and energy. It is through this vibration that the soul contacts spirit. Individuality should be fostered by religion, not discouraged. The road to the Kingdom of God is not a singular course; there are many ways to reach it. Consider the simple analogy of two people living in a suburb of a large metropolitan area. Both are instructed to travel to the same destination and arrive at an agreed upon time. Although they depart from the same point of origin, they decide to travel their own individual routes. Each will arrive at the same destination. The length and intensity of the journey may prove to be different; yet they will both arrive at the appointed place. Although very simplistic, the analogy is worth consideration. There are many roads to travel in the realm of spirit. The correct path for any soul is the one that is consciously chosen to travel. It is along the chosen path that spirit will manifest itself to the seeker.

By limiting oneself to the ideas of others, the seeker surrenders its true power and potential. The intensity of *Light* the soul generates is diminished, and the universe is affected. I am not stating that all clergy members foster a lust for power and self-importance. There are many wonderful souls that are guiding their followers, encouraging them to shine their

Light as brightly as they can. When souls align themselves with such a wonderful leader, then they should glean all the life and wisdom that is being offered. Embrace those who encourage enlightenment and love. Absorb the energy they exude. However, there are many that have become deluded by power and impose dogma upon their congregation. Beware of such leaders.

G: I can understand what you have just described. I had been heavily indoctrinated by dogma as a young child and have lived many years in blindness. You had stated that there are other reasons that the rational mind does not "see" the world of spirit. Would you please elaborate on the others?

Chief: There are volumes that could be spoken on this issue, but I will explain only one more. The rational mind of the scientist is often the reason many souls do not recognize the existence of spirit.

G: I had the feeling you were going there next. May I state my opinion regarding this area before you elaborate upon your philosophy?

Chief: Of course you may. You are as much spirit as I am. Your thoughts, as are the thoughts of all souls, are honored in the universe. What is it that you have to say regarding science and spirit?

G: I will say this. For many years I have taught my students the fundamental beliefs of ancient civilizations. Included in this

The Chief

instruction are units on Greek and Roman mythology. I have long been fascinated by the stories created by these ancient peoples. Some are quite difficult to believe, especially those that explain the origin of natural occurrences. I'm quite certain that spiders are truly not the result of Athena's confrontation with the disrespectful Arcane. I seriously doubt that the quarrel among Athena, Aphrodite, and Hera resulted in the battles of the Trojan War, nor do I believe that snakes came to inhabit the desert when the Medusa's blood dripped from the pouch carried by Perseus when he flew overhead on Pegasus. Science easily disproves these theories.

However, what truly fascinates me is that each of these ancient civilizations harbored the concept of a higher power. I am amazed at how the perspective of deities has changed over the course of time. I recognize that although the concept of spirit has changed in the way we consider its existence, the basic concept remains imbedded in the soul of the human being. Most humans bear an inherent belief in a higher power. How this power is defined and interpreted is widely debated. However, it seems to be an inherent part of our being.

Now, the mythical origins of the earth's atmospheric and topographic wonders have been proven to be the result of folly by the world of science, and justifiably so. The function of the earth, the space above and beyond, and the human body has been highly scrutinized by science, and the old myths have been proven to be simply what the word implies. My personal opinion is that the world of seekers who blindly believe in the power and intercession of God to care for their every need has become a highly naïve place of existence. An example of this would be the parent who denies his gravely ill child the benefits of modern medicine and trusts that God will solely cure his child. The parent is doing injustice to the child. However, perhaps the parent of that child might consider that God has guided him toward the appropriate medical treatment. Yet this is where the arrogance of the scientist sometimes manifests itself. The scientist is aware of the inner workings of the human body, yet how many physicians are unable to properly diagnose the root of a medical condition? In this day and age, it seems that when a physician cannot readily diagnose the cause of an illness, the simplest explanation is stress. Perhaps stress might be analogous to Arachne's plight. Perhaps certain illnesses are the result of a spiritual origin. Perhaps there exists a duality between science and spirit. The scientist has his definite ideas, as does the spiritualist. Perhaps when the two are combined, then the truth will be known.

Chief: Your ideas are well founded, my friend. You are understanding the evolutionary process that is taking place in the universe right now regarding the development of your planet. The scientist is an extremely powerful component to the world's development. The spiritualist exists in an equally important capacity. When the consciousness of man truly comprehends the relationship of science and spirit, then man will be able to use all his resources to create a harmonious world. This potential truly exists.

However, there are factors that impede this development from manifesting itself fully. The greatest factor that impedes this progress is the human spirit itself. The mind's ego and lusts are detrimental to the fulfillment of man's potential. Many humans separate themselves from one another through selfish thinking and deeds. Many humans are held captive by those who control them through economic, political, and religious means. Many are separated through ignorance of things that exist outside of their immediate society. There are many reasons that man demonstrates inhumanity toward man. Yet the potential for harmony does exist in the soul of each human who inhabits your planet. *Darkness* must be balanced with *Light* for harmony to occur. This is why it is essential for those who understand the *Light* to allow theirs to shine as brightly as possible. It is very important and most essential. Let your *Light* shine brightly, not only for yourself but also for the good of all creation. This is a sacred truth.

G: Are there secrets to overcoming the ego and lusts?

Chief: There are no secrets in the universe. The truth is available for all who seek it.

G: Many readers might find this simplicity difficult to believe. Can you advise them as to how to access the truth?

Chief: I have just done so by stating that truth is available to those who seek it. Simply ask, and it will be revealed. Scriptures instruct us to knock and our call will be answered. This is truly how spirit works. However, when people become interested in finding the truth, then they must be willing to change their perception of life in some ways. When something is gained, then something must be lost. I am referring to certain thought patterns and longings of the soul. Many individuals try very hard to overcome the obstacles of their ego and desire but are not completely dedicated to changing their pattern of vibration.

G: I understand this, Chief. I truly do. I understand that enlightenment is a journey, a process that takes time to absorb and recognize. Thank you for your revelations. Are there any more insights that you wish to share?

Chief: Yes, there is one more I would like to discuss, a very important issue regarding enlightenment. The issue to which I am referring is judgment. Learn to judge no one, for as you judge so will you be judged.

When a soul passes judgment on another, then he is diminishing the amount of *Light* being generated into the universe. By judging others we are merely affirming our personal positions in the universe. A truly enlightened soul learns to leave the judgments to God. This is not always a simple skill to master, but one that is worth the effort. It can be learned when people realize that the mind functions best as a tool of the soul.

G: I think I understand what you are saying, but would you please articulate the thought a bit more?

Chief: Certainly. You see, the mind is a powerful tool, an incredible tool. The mind is capable of creating greatness, and also of destroying greatness. If the mind is left uncontrolled by the spirit, by the insight of functioning for the highest good of all of creation, then the mind might not exert the control necessary to function for the good of the universe. Terrible thoughts can create terrible circumstances. Greed, lust, envy, and hatred are the products of the mind, not the spirit. Peace, love, compassion, and harmony are products of the mind as well. When one learns to control his or her thoughts through the soul, then the mind will function on a spiritual level. This is an easy concept to understand, yet difficult to master. However, mastery is achieved through the process of trial and error, through active seeking and practice. As I've mentioned earlier, there are guides available to those who seek guidance in mastering the mind. All one must do to access these guides is call them from the heart. The call will be heard, and guides will come forward to assist the soul who seeks them.

G: You've taught me a great deal on that subject already. I am learning to apply your teachings to my life. Please explain to the readers the simplest way to master the mind.

Chief: Of course I will. It is quite simple. Learn to recognize destructive thoughts and simply eliminate them from your consciousness. The way I teach this is that when a destructive thought is recognized, simply tell it that it does not exist for the highest good of all creation and it must dissipate. When we realize that our individual existence is a part of all that exists, that individual endeavors are really traps, then it becomes easier for the soul to master the mind. The realization that positive energy will create more positive energy will cause the soul to seek thoughts of finer vibration. Thus a new thought process is developed, one that will generate power. The soul may then realize that it is a vessel of *Light*. It is then able to receive the gifts that the universe offers on a constant basis with the realization that the more we receive, the more we are capable of giving. It is when the receiving becomes more important than the giving that the receiving will diminish. Allow your spirit to absorb this statement, and you will understand its simplicity and truth.

G: How does judgment affect this truth?

Chief: When people judge they are seeking to empower and validate themselves. They are thinking selfishly, not in terms of all creation. Learn to judge no one. Learn to recognize the negativity of the act. Allow your soul to instruct your mind to think universally. It is in this mastery that the course of your world's development can be altered. Thoughts are more powerful than actions, for actions are the result of thoughts. Thoughts emanated through spirit are necessary for your planet, and the entire world of all creation. Learn to think properly, learn to control your mind. Keep your focus on what is greater than the self is, and it can be done.

There is one more insight I would like to offer regarding judgment. Do not judge yourself, for in doing so you weaken your energy. By weakening your energy, you weaken the entire universe. Self-judgment often produces weakness in souls, particularly when this judgment is the result of measuring oneself against others. Souls often observe the accomplishments of others and feel insecure about what they themselves have not accomplished. This is a waste of spiritual energy. A wise soul will rejoice in the success of others, for each success is a success for the highest good of all creation. Always value yourself and understand the strengths and gifts

The Chief

that make you who you are. Celebrate the strength of others as well as your own. Envy and self-doubt are symptoms of weakness, and there is no need for any soul to feel that way. Encourage your spirit to instruct your mind to dwell on your value to the universe, whatever it might be. The universe views all souls as equals; it is the individual soul that sometimes does not comprehend this truth. No soul is greater than another in the eyes of spirit. Celebrate your strength, and learn strength from others as well. Shine your *Light* brightly, for the universe needs whatever *Light* you are willing to offer. Think through your soul, and your mind will produce experiences far beyond what it has ever imagined. Comprehend this truth, both for yourself and for the highest good of all creation.

There are many more truths to be revealed to you and all beings of your planet. However, those that I have revealed must suffice for the moment. Absorb the lessons I have offered, and use this knowledge to benefit yourself and all of God's creation. Be wise, and you will help your planet flourish.

G: Chief, I have waited a long time for your voice to reach me once again. The reader will not understand that we had become estranged for more than six months, for whatever reasons there were. Yet I called and you rushed to speak with me. I am most grateful to you for the ways that you have enhanced my life, my spirit, and my existence. Thank you so much for your unselfish and nonjudgmental response. You have taught your lessons well. You will forever remain a part of my world.

Chief: It is my great joy to share insights with you, my friend. It is my fervent wish that all those reading this work will become empowered with *Light*.

G: As all spirits are doing, would you please conclude our session with a final thought?

Chief: Love is the true power of the universe. Love all creation because you are part of all creation. Learn to allow your spirit to guide your thoughts. Take your cosmic responsibility seriously, and empower yourself with *Light*. Life is an individual journey, yet you need not walk alone. Surround yourself with those who understand love, and your soul will shine brightly. May the peace of understanding fill your spirit for all eternity. May you simply know love.

G: Thank you, Chief. From the depth of my soul, I thank you. You are a true friend. I will forever be grateful.

Chief: *Na-ho-tae,. Sha-no-hey.* My blessings to all.

Mamma Soul

Rightful Thinking

Mamma Soul is someone that I had heard of many years ago but did not take the time to know. I don't quite remember the year. It was perhaps 1969 or a year or two before or after. I do, however, recall the exact spot in which I actually felt her presence. I was in New Haven, Connecticut; I was driving my car on Crescent St., and when I reached the intersection of The Boulevard a song came on the radio that spoke of Mamma Soul. She immediately intrigued me, and I wished that I could know her. A verse of the song went: "Son, never you mind, just sing from your soul." That lyric penetrated my being immediately.

However, at that particular time in my life, I had very little spiritual awareness or aptitude. I was living recklessly and blindly. My soul longed to know her at that moment, but I felt that she would never care to speak to me. It's taken over thirty years for me to realize that, had I invited her into my life at that particular moment, she would have obliged me gladly. However, the time for us to communicate was not at hand. Hearing her voice so long after is a valuable lesson that I can share. Spirit is always available if we seek it. It will not necessarily seek us, but it will always answer our call. Knock and the door will be opened. It's a very simple truth.

Having stated the circumstances of our knowing each other, I will invite Mamma Soul to share with you her very special and enlightening insights. I am truly grateful that she has manifested herself in my life.

* * *

G: Greetings, Mamma Soul. Thank you so much for sharing yourself with me and those who are reading this book. I am grateful for your guidance.

Mamma Soul: Greetings to you also, my young friend. I am sincerely happy to be sharing my thoughts with you. Now don't you be worrying about what is to be said and written. Don't you be worried at all. Just speak with me plainly and truthfully. You and many other souls of the earth spend too much time concerning yourself with the foolish notion that what you say and do might not measure up to the standards of others. Your work is one of beauty, for you are simply revealing truths to those who care to listen. So lighten up your spirit, and talk to Mamma Soul with a happy heart. Do you hear?

G: Yes, I hear you and will follow your advice. I will listen to all you wish to say.

Mamma Soul: That is a wonderful thing to do, and a very difficult one, I might add. The majority of souls inhabiting your planet are not very good listeners. They listen very selectively for what will benefit them. Many only feign listening, merely awaiting their turn to express their ideas. A true listener is a very unique individual. Listening is a most important skill. One learns much more by listening than they do by speaking, you know.

G: I've heard that before, and I do understand its merit. My problem, if I might express myself honestly, is that by listening many opportunities are lost. It seems that one needs to be aggressive to succeed in earth's environment.

Mamma Soul: You are speaking quite without wisdom right now, and I am surprised. I am not disappointed, for I am not judgmental in any way. Perhaps your statement was one expressed by the energy of others who are without understanding of their place in the universe. Assuming so, I will speak of circumstances for those who are in need of an explanation.

To begin, success is a very personal definition. Right now you may be referring to being recognized for your talents. That certainly would be an expression of success. However, that is very personal. You've heard other spirits speak of the number of souls inhabiting your planet, their varied energies, and their vast differences. So you must be careful, you know, when applying your personal definitions toward the population at large. I will offer you a very simple statement. Success is merely succeeding at what you wish to be successful at. Do you understand that statement?

G: Yes, I do understand. I suppose it's safe to say that success is merely a personal perception.

Mamma Soul: Yes, you are correct. That is good. The next thing to consider is what one does with success. That is a crucial matter for the entire universe. Do you know what I am saying, young friend?

G: I do. I've heard it before and am not surprised that you are saying it once again.

Mamma Soul: Do not be surprised, for all spirits that speak with you have at least one commonality in their messages. Whatever you achieve, do so for the highest good of all creation. That is important, for all creation is a part of the great energy, the energy of the Creator. There are many names for the Creator, for there are many different cultures and religions that exist in the universe. My personal name for the Creator is God. It's not the name that is significant—it's the understanding of the one Great Energy that is a part of all beings of the universe.

Now, no soul is more important than another. Some spirits do accomplish more than others, and for many reasons. Yet any heart that beats for the sake of all creation is adding to the *Light* necessary to sustain the spirit of God. Any soul that exists to help the entire universe is an ally of the greatest spirit of all. That is why souls should never allow disappointment to shroud their worth to the energy of spirit. When the dust settles, as many humans use as a metaphor for reflection, the only thing that truly matters is the *Light* and love one generates into the universe for the good of all creation. All the wondrous deeds one might accomplish, all the recognition one might receive, will disperse like dust in the wind if accomplishments were achieved in a selfish vein. Only deeds performed and executed for the good of all creation will remain known in the energy of *Light*.

G: You refer to the energy of *Light*. Is there truly an energy of *Darkness*?

Mamma Soul: Yes, young friend, there is. Most souls recognize this within their hearts, if not in their thoughts. There is an energy that opposes *Light*; *Darkness* is the absence of *Light*. Those who exist outside of the *Light*, who turn their awareness away from it, exist in *Darkness*. It is here that many deeds and accomplishments are recalled also. However these deeds are recognized, they will not be a part of God. Even temples built in the Creator's name will not be recognized by the universe of *Light* if they are erected without love of all of creation. This is a very simple truth, and one that must be considered by spirits of all dimensions who seek the *Light*. Do everything that you do in the spirit of all creation. It is not a difficult task if you take the time to consider its power, consider its truth.

G: Other spirits have shared insights regarding this. It seems to be a universal truth. Is this so?

Mamma Soul: Of course it is, my friend. Why else would all who are enlightened share this truth? It is very important to dedicate our actions to the good of all of creation for, once again, all of creation is a part of God. Knowing this makes people of your planet true brothers and sisters. You, as are all spirits, are a part of the family of God. However, not all families function well. Any human can understand this. In many families there is bitterness, there are hostilities.

G: How would you explain this?

Mamma Soul: Very simply. It is because the selfish and self-centered ego is ruling the mind.

G: Please elaborate, Mamma Soul.

Mamma Soul: Of course. You see, the selfish ego is a part of mankind that separates members of the species. Of course there are inherited traits, along with cultural and environmental differences that cause separation to some extent, but the true culprit of hostility is the selfish ego. It is because of the selfish ego that humans bring suffering to the planet. It is because of the selfish ego that wars are fought, crimes are committed, and atrocities are inflicted on fellow members of the human race. It is because of the selfish ego that jealousy is empowered. It is because of the selfish ego that one feels more or less powerful than others. The selfish ego is a tool of destruction and a product of wrongful thinking.

Now I know you'll be asking, how does one defeat and control the selfish, self-centered ego? And I know you'll be understanding my answer. It is through correct thinking that the ego is controlled. It is through raising the consciousness that the individual realizes the power of rightful thinking and the responsibility to think rightfully. The selfish ego can then be transformed into the selfless ego and become an instrument of the *Light*.

I suppose I should express my thoughts a bit more clearly. *Rightful* really means *proper* to you. You must think in a proper manner, and the proper manner is to keep in mind that each and every one of us is a part of all creation. Thinking in this manner reveals a very simple truth: we are all true brethren because we are all filled with the Creator's spirit. We are united in our souls because each and every soul contains the Creator's spirit within it. We all possess the free will to choose to recognize or ignore this energy that dwells within us, but the truth is that we all possess this energy within our souls. Of course I am saying this very often in our conversation, but I say only important things to you. This is my message and my enlightened contribution to your work. Think properly. It is your right, as well as your obligation.

G: I do understand what you have to say. I, and many others of the earth, do honestly try to think rightfully, as you have called it. Yet it is so difficult to do so all the time. I truly wish that I could, but there are so many conflicting circumstances that deter me from staying on the path.

Mamma Soul: This is not to be denied. Of course it is difficult. Why would it not be so? Understand that your earthly existence deals many trials to the human. It is a part of the experience of living on your planet. You are not expected to be perfect, but you certainly have the potential to be so. There are among you many who have evolved into perfection. Enlightenment is a process. Only a few designated souls are born enlightened into the human condition. There are many notable prophets who have walked your planet and have revealed the truth of the Great Energy. And those prophets who have performed miracles have offered you the same message. All is possible in the energy of God. The words and energy of these great and enlightened prophets continue to exist for thousands of years, even after their physical bodies have departed from earth. Their lives were lived so that humans will have a tangible example of how they too may live.

Heed the messages of those who have lived their lives in order to offer you insights of how you may live yours as well. Each prophet has offered you the message that you too are capable of great deeds, of performing miracles. The truth of existence lies within each of us, no matter how we exist in the universe. We all possess the potential to dwell in the *Light*. It is our free will to choose where we wish to dwell. We can choose to exist as close to or as far away from the *Light* as we do. Choose the *Light*, choose to dwell in the energy of the great Creator, and all things will become possible. Think of this for a moment, and you will understand its truth.

G: You make it sound very simple, but I know from experience that it is not such an easy task. Would you please offer some insight as to how one can master the skill of rightful thinking?

Mamma Soul: Of course. The most important key to rightful thinking is to have the desire to think this way. True desire is the most important ingredient. Once true desire is established in the heart, then one must understand that it becomes a process. Some find the process relatively easy to master; others find it extremely difficult. The speed at which one masters rightful thinking is not important. It is the process itself and the benefit that the universe receives that is most important.

Here is a simple analogy to make this statement more clear. Consider a person whose body has become depleted of its strength through abuse. The individual has resolved many times to change his ways and to take action to restore his body to health and beauty. Many feeble attempts are made toward improvement but are eventually abandoned because the abusive behavior of this individual is stronger than the desire to improve. However, a moment arrives within this individual when he recognizes the true value of strengthening his body. It could be for a variety of reasons that the insight becomes empowered, but the insight becomes the motivation to improve, and this person sets out to do so in earnest. Conditioning might be very difficult at first, and results might be slow to see and feel. But this does not discourage the individual enough to abandon his journey. Although many discouraging moments may enter his psyche, he endures at whatever pace he can, for he knows that the ultimate goal is mastery of his body. There will arrive a time in his journey when this individual takes a moment to reflect on how far he has come, how much he has changed. He will understand how he has progressed since the inception of his conditioning regimen. Of course there might be moments of temporary lapses, but this individual will continue to condition his body because he has tasted the success of his desire. He will return to the path that makes him feel whole.

The same is true of rightful thinking. It is very difficult for some, for many have chosen to think wrongfully for such a long time in their lives. Thoughts of anger, jealousy, hatred, greed, and lust have become deeply embedded in the mind and a habitual way of thinking. Changing these thought processes is not an easy task for many. However, should an individual develop the true desire to change his or her way of thinking, then all he or she must do is tell the universe of this desire and change will be set in motion. It might be discouraging at first, for wrongful thoughts may not wish to be abandoned so easily. However, if the individual keeps in mind that rightful thinking benefits the entire universe and not only himself, then it becomes an easier task to perform. Rightful thinking makes one a true child of God. It is more powerful than the performance of good deeds done with the purpose of winning the favor of God, trying only to secure a favorable place in the Creator's eyes. Rightful thinking opens the door to love, and love is all God asks of us. If one understands love, then one will function as a part of the Creator.

This is a truth, my friend, a very sacred truth. Ask whatever form of deity that is natural to you for help in developing rightful thinking. Become vigilant in your desire. Yes, you will experience many moments of frustration because negative thoughts are powerful and *Darkness* is not quick to surrender those who perpetuate its energy. When moments of weakness will not allow you peace, when your mind swims with wrongful thoughts, reach into your soul for strength. Speak with the guiding forces of the universe. Recognize this moment as it is, a moment of wrongful thinking. Understand that this moment, like all moments in the universe, will pass. A dreadful storm is usually followed by beautiful skies.

G: I truly understand your message, Mamma Soul. Do others hear you also?

Mamma Soul: Many others hear me and spirits like me, although not in the same voice that you do. There are infinite ways to hear the voice of spirit. Humans should understand that they too are spirits and messages that they generate from the *Light* are spiritual messages as well. Do not concern yourself with who believes you. Do not worry that what you say might be construed as nonsense. Do not worry about a single thing, for as long as you place yourself in the hands of God and commit yourself to contributing to the *Light*, then all that you need will manifest itself to you.

G: I comprehend your statement, truly. However, your statement fosters a question in my mind. I construe your insights as true insights of spirit. I feel them in my soul, and they are very real to me. Yet there are many who hear the voice of spirit and interpret these voices in ways that promote violence and imposition of one's will upon the will of another. Why is this so?

Mamma Soul: That is an age-old question, my friend. It is also one that is not so easy to answer. You see, forces of *Darkness*, forces that exist outside the energy of *Light*, are very powerful. They are potent and dangerous. They are constantly attempting to steal from the *Light*. *Darkness* often attaches itself to those who are weak in energy and vulnerable to the promises of a fuller existence if they follow blindly. Finding the *Light* must become an individual choice. When one discovers the *Light*, then he realizes that violence committed against his neighbor is outside the forces of love. Acts of greed and violence contribute to disharmony in the universe.

A love of the forces of *Darkness* captures the soul that is living outside the forces of *Light*. Love for all creation will remove one from this kind of thinking. Unfortunately, not all possess the wisdom to perceive that they are living in blindness and will do much to cause hardship for their brethren. It is a natural part of the universal energy. *Light* and *Darkness* exist throughout the entire universe, in all dimensions of creation. When one accesses the concept of true love then he will know who preaches false ideas. The true answer is that the heart must speak, not the mind. The truth of *Light* is found in one's heart and soul. All one must do is seek the *Light*, for the knowledge of love dwells inherently within us all.

G: That is an incredible insight. It's also frightening in ways.

Mamma Soul: Do not be frightened, my friend, for if you are existing in the realm of God's love then there is no need for anxiety. Recognize the *Darkness*, understand and respect its presence and power, and actively choose the *Light*. Seek the masters of the *Light*, and all you need will be provided for you. Resolve to use the power gained though your insights for the highest good of all creation. It truly is not complicated. Complications arise in the mind; simplicity arises in the soul.

G: How does one truly live from the soul?

Mamma Soul: Living through the soul is the essential ingredient to proper existence. For some it is very natural, for others quite unnatural. It can be learned, as all things can be learned. If you find this concept of living from your soul unnatural, then you must take time as often as possible to seek a quiet moment to access the depths of your soul. There are many ways to do this. Some call it meditation, which is a most appropriate term. However, there are many among you who tell themselves that they are incapable of properly meditating, thinking wrongly that this is a kind of magical practice. Those selling the idea would have one believe this is so.

Listen to me carefully. Hear Mamma Soul. Take time whenever possible to listen to the depth of your soul. Allow yourself to be still, and you will hear it. Practice being still, not in your body but in your mind. The voice of stillness can be heard in the depth of your being. When you have learned to be still, learn to listen to the inner voice that directs you. Do not analyze what you hear, simply listen. Understand that the true voice of the *Light* speaks of selfless love, a love that helps you to recognize yourself as a true brethren to all of mankind. Knowing this will help you discriminate between the voice of the selfish ego and the voice of love. When you have learned to listen, then you must learn to believe. That is the most difficult part of the process for most humans. Humans are so busy most of the time, attempting to accomplish so much, that they rarely take the time to reflect on the true meaning of existence. The true meaning of existence is to be one with the Creator.

G: That is such a beautiful insight, yet I sometimes find it difficult to execute. It sometimes seems like a lot of work to be still. Can you help me with this?

Mamma Soul: Of course. Understand this concept. You inhabit your planet more than once. You do so many times, for your soul is constantly evolving. There are other dimensions apart from earth, but I am here to address those of earth's dimension. Each time a soul inhabits the earth, a new learning experience is offered to the soul. As a soul evolves in spiritual awareness, then finding the stillness becomes much easier, for the soul is wiser to the purpose of existence. One should never be discouraged by their supposed inability to access the stillness, for there is no rush in the universe. All is delivered in its proper time. Each moment is special in its own way. When a soul learns how to be one with the Creator's energy, then he or she will understand that enlightenment has been discovered. It is at this moment that the soul will choose how to continue its journey.

I understand that this will sound like nonsense to some who read this. That too is a part of the developmental process of spirit. There are some who will read and understand this insight but resist it, for they feel incapable of applying the principle to their existence. But it will be felt in their soul, and that may become the beginning of their enlightened journey. There are still others who will read and smile from their souls, for they will understand that their knowing is indeed true.

All of creation exists together. All of creation is capable of accessing the Creator's energy. It is accessed through surrender and love. Remember this truth. It is my gift to you.

G: Mamma Soul, thank you so much for the insights you have revealed. You have been waiting patiently to speak with me for thirty years. I find that in itself incredible. You have taught me so much, and I am sincerely grateful. Would you please deliver your final insight to all of us who are hearing your voice?

Mamma Soul: Of course, my friend. That is precisely why I have come forward. My final advice to you all is to surrender your spirit to the spirit of the Creator. Relax in the Creator's love. Laugh as much as possible, and know that all you do is for the highest good of all creation. Be a part of God, for God is a natural part of us all. Simply ask God to enter, and *He* or *She* will touch you. Listen through your own soul, and you will understand all that needs to be understood. Relax and allow life to happen. That is all one needs to do.

It is with great pleasure that I communicate with you. Mamma Soul will always be here for you, and for anyone who needs me. May the Creator's energy tickle your soul. Blessings to all!

Haitukulu

Matters of Soul

Haitukulu is a wizard, a true and bona fide wizard. In fact, he is my ideal when it comes to wizards. I first saw Haitukulu circa 1971. I was riding my motorcycle down Main St. in Babylon, New York. Babylon is a small but bustling town on Long Island. While stopped at a traffic light, I glanced toward the old nursing home across the street. There was a large porch on the building, and an empty bench caught my attention. However, to my surprise, I saw an image of an old, bearded man seated there! I knew that he was not a physical man, yet I saw this kindly, wise man staring out at me. At the time I was twenty-two years old and filled with testosterone and a mind for letting the good times roll. Spiritual inclination had not yet become a part of my consciousness. However, I just stared at the vision of this being and knew he existed for some reason. I simply knew this was a guide of some sort, even though my mind had not engaged in such a concept before. It was simply a "knowing" inside of me that I had no rational idea about. I later "met" him when I was writing one of my favorite stories, "Morris Lararby's Dream

Machine." Haitukulu appeared as the Dream Wizard, and I have revered him ever since.

To be honest, I did not think that he would manifest himself in this work until much later in its composition, but he has chosen to come forward at this moment in time. I must tell you that he is incredibly special to me and that he is unlike any wizard I have ever imagined. He is incredibly benevolent and caring, and in my mind is a deity of sorts. His existence has been a very important part of my own for quite some time now, and my respect for him is immeasurable. He needs no further introduction, for I have no words to describe him properly. He is simply a master.

* * *

Haitukulu

G: Greetings, Haitukulu. Thank you so much for coming forward. I must begin by telling you that I am bit intimidated to be speaking with you. You have been both my idol and ideal for so long now, and I am very shy to actually speak to you.

Haitukulu: Thank you for your kind words of introduction. I also understand your feelings of awe, for I have known you for quite some time now. Your reverence is appreciated, but not necessary. However, your reverence is a fine quality and one that is a part of your soul. And that is precisely why I have chosen to come forward at this time. I've come to address the issue of soul.

G: I am very excited that you have chosen to do so at this time. Issues of soul are what have been very much on my mind.

Haitukulu: That is exactly why I am here. You have called, and I have answered. It's the way of spirit. However, let us not discuss this on a personal level. I am here to reveal things to all who care to listen. My message is for everyone who cares to understand.

G: I agree with you. I am tempted to address you as Master, but I have a feeling that you would reject the title.

Haitukulu: You are correct; I would prefer that you refrain from referring to me as Master. I have mastered much in my existence, yet my mastery is not something that I need or want attached to my name. Whatever I have learned is in the interest of all creation. The term Master is reserved to those who truly are deities. All parts of creation possess mastery within their souls. Some have learned to recognize it while others choose to allow their mastery to remain dormant.

G: We choose to let our mastery lie dormant?

Haitukulu: Precisely. In matters of soul, we all choose the level at which we exist. It is not a very difficult concept to understand once the soul chooses to face itself. Life at all levels of existence is a matter of soul. It is our soul that connects each of us to the great energy we call God. It is our soul that makes us God. It is our soul that is the image and likeness of God that many religions refer to. There are many words and terms used to describe this energy, many perceptions of who He/She is. However, words are not important, for words are not necessary when it comes to communicating with the Great Energy. God is reached through the soul. All one must do is look within the soul, and all of creation can be found.

G: You make it sound very simple to do this. Is it really that easy?

Haitukulu: Like all things, it is easy once one learns the methods of doing so. Is using the computer on which you are writing on easy for you?

G: Certain applications are. There are many things I do not know and understand regarding this computer, but I suppose I can learn.

Haitukulu: You have expressed yourself very well. Once you learn more applications on your computer, they will become easy for you to execute. You must seek ways to learn these applications. Keep in mind that how you learn may be quite different from the way others will learn the same things. Some do well by learning on their own; others seek teachers to guide them. Still others will read material and apply it. There are so many ways to decide how to learn to use your computer, and the rate and method of your learning is up to you.

Keep in mind that all applications exist even if you do not realize that they do. The more you learn, the more you will come to understand that there is even more to learn. However, you can draw on past experiences to assist you in understanding new applications. Experience is a wonderful teacher. The same is true of spirit. There is much to learn; probably more than you even know exists. However, all can be learned and mastered if one allows the soul to explore spirit. There are no true mysteries, although most humans choose to believe there to be so. Spiritual awareness is an evolutionary process, and the only limits to understanding spiritual principles are the limits the soul creates for itself.

G: What are the best methods to understanding spirit?

Haitukulu: Once again, that is quite a personal question. There is no single method. Energy is so diverse; there are so many energies and so many different frequencies of vibration. It would be very difficult to prescribe a single method of soul development. However, there are a few simple techniques that are common to all souls who are seeking to connect to the true energy of spirit. The first is meditation.

Meditation is a difficult concept for many humans, yet it need not be so. There have been many self-proclaimed masters who have sold their techniques to seekers, creating an aura of mystique. This type of presentation often creates anxiety for those seeking the benefits of the meditative process. Again, the ability to mediate is contained within every soul; souls merely have to learn to relax. Unfortunately, many souls are so busy and so filled with anxiety that relaxation of the mind is a very difficult chore. However, it need not be.

G: I have learned that concept. I have often found relaxing my mind a difficult task. Would you please share a few simple insights as to how this relaxed state of mind can be achieved?

Haitukulu: Most certainly, it will be my pleasure. The first thing one must do is desire to learn to access spirit. A call must be made through the soul. Many do not realize or believe this simple spiritual principle. All one must do is ask, and spirit will respond. Once the call is made, then energy is set in motion. Novices in the ways of spirit might be looking for a grandiose reaction from spirit, and this might actually come to pass in the form of an event or apparition of someone significant. All is possible, yet spirit is usually more subtle in its working. The process of soul development is exactly that, a process. A virtuoso pianist does not perform at a major venue without years of practice and development. Prodigies do exist, yet they are not the norm and are an entity that could be discussed at length. However, I am deviating from the original question and wish to remain on task.

Once the desire to understand spirit is made from the soul, then the soul will seek ways to be connected. It is then that the soul will relax its focus from the busy activities of the individual and the anxious thoughts of the mind. A few moments of simply being still in the mind will begin to become manifest, and it is in these moments of stillness that the soul will begin to train the mind. Most human minds have learned to be so active due to the influences of society, especially those who dwell in Western and capitalistic ways of life. Thoughts run rampant through the mind and often become entangled in a web of constant movement. The soul that becomes enlightened, at any level, begins to control the mind and learns how to create silence.

One must understand that the process may take time, more than some are willing to invest. Meditation is learned a step at a time, much like walking on two legs is for the human being. Like walking, once the process is understood, the soul will not forget. Learn to quiet your mind, and learn to listen. These are very simple, yet difficult, tasks. However, if the soul seeks in earnest to learn meditation, then it will do so.

G: I understand what you have said and have learned to access the stillness, although I do need to develop my skills further. You had used the word *methods* when you began your explanation of learning the ways of spirit. Meditation is one. Are there others?

Haitukulu: Indeed there are others. I will limit my explanation to the most simple and comprehensible. Another method of developing the soul's power is through prayer. As in meditation, there are numerous ways to pray and numerous concepts regarding prayer. My suggestion is that one prays in the manner in which one is most comfortable. However, I will issue one caution. The process of blindly reciting words without faith in their power will be rendered useless in the universe. Better to just speak from the heart than to blindly follow a formula that has been prescribed by others.

G: I am tempted to ask a naïve question here regarding prayer and what you have just described. I will refrain from asking and allow you to continue.

Haitukulu: The question you would ask, on behalf of those who might be confused, would imply that it might be somewhat blasphemous to ignore the sacred words of a proven religion. I can surely understand this. However, think for a moment. Prayers that have stood the test of time, that have been recited over and over for centuries, are certainly words of power. How else could they have survived the test of time? However, what has empowered them has been the manner in which they are prayed.

    This is a relatively simple concept to understand at any level of intellectual scrutiny. When people use structured prayers as a means to communicate with spirit, then they will be effective, so long as they are prayed from the heart. Yet they are not the only prayers that are recognized in the universe. Spirit recognizes all calls from the heart. The heart and soul are the centers of power in the universe. It is the soul that influences the heart and the mind. It is the soul that connects all spirits to the universal spirit of God. So do not hesitate to speak with deities in any words that come from your heart and are initiated by the soul. All prayer is heard in the universe. It is a natural law.

G: I understand that all prayer is heard, but is all prayer answered?

Haitukulu: The answer to your question is yes, all prayer is answered. However, that is a rather ambiguous response, for all prayers are not always answered in satisfaction for what has been asked. Simply stated, the answers to prayers might not be what the soul has asked for. Yet prayers will be answered once they are prayed. That is a universal principle.

G: My personal experience regarding prayer is that my prayers take a long time to be answered. Why is that?

Haitukulu: It is because that is your belief.

G: I'm not sure that I understand this explanation.

Haitukulu: Your soul needs time to ready itself for the response to your prayers. Your spirit is filled with caution, and understanding takes time for you to develop. It is simply the way your soul functions at this moment in time. However, what is true for you is not necessarily true for another. Prayer is a very personal experience, and how and when prayers are answered are up to each individual's soul. It is important to understand this statement: response to prayer is proportionate to the amount of faith a soul exerts into prayer.

Also, the time that spirit takes to respond to prayer is insignificant, for in reality time is irrelevant. Life is eternal, and all moments are a part of eternity. The answer to all prayer exists in all moments; it is up to the soul to discover it. It might take a moment to comprehend this statement. However, if you think clearly you will understand that what I have described is true. Allow your rational mind to absorb the statement, and you will understand its truth. I have stressed the word *moment* quite a bit in my explanation and have done so for a specific reason.

Life, at every level of existence, is the process of living in the present moment. Ponder this statement, and you will understand its validity. Your mind and soul harbor many memories of days passed, some with pleasant feelings, others with consternation. You dream of days to come and create visions of your future. Yet the place from which you reflect and dream is the present, the now. We exist merely in the moment, and if the soul recognizes the power of living in the moment, it will create a powerful future. Every moment in time offers souls an opportunity to erase mistakes made along their journeys and to create new beginnings for productive futures. Recognizing the reality of the present moment is a skill that can be learned, one that can be mastered. Prayer and meditation are vital tools regarding this mastery. Each soul that seeks enlightenment should invest time into understanding the significance of mastering the present moment and these vehicles, or any vehicle that might increase awareness.

Haitukulu

G: I comprehend what you have described. I have experienced the power of prayer and meditation at moments in my life. Are there other components involved in the process of enlightenment?

Haitukulu: Yes, there are. One of the most important components, as you describe it, is faith. Faith in an incredibly powerful part of the soul. It is faith that can "move mountains." It is faith that creates miracles. It is faith that empowers the soul to achieve, to understand. It is faith that fuels the soul. Truly, nothing is impossible to one who believes.

G: I am intrigued by the power of faith. Is it something that can be developed?

Haitukulu: Most certainly. Faith does not always come easily to the soul. Many individuals need to see to believe. They may pray: "If you could just show me a sign, I will believe with all my heart." It most likely will take a soul in this stage of development a long while to come to understand the validity and power of faith. Yet that is perfectly acceptable, for all things are revealed in the moments in which they are destined to become manifest. The rate at which a soul develops its understanding of faith is an individual process. The soul must first recognize what it seeks to have faith in. This may involve a great deal of searching for some, while to others it is a very natural process. That is why it is important for seekers to be cautious about comparing themselves to others. As stated before, life is an individual journey. We have much to learn from others, yet the process of life is our own. It is wise to choose our own beliefs and to create our own communion with the universal spirit. Each of us is a special and unique part of the Creator. Having faith in ourselves is a way of honoring spirit.

G: Thank you for such a beautiful description of the power of faith. I do, however, have a question regarding faith. Is blind faith constructive or destructive to the soul?

Haitukulu: You have posed a powerful question. It is possible to be both constructive and destructive, again depending on the heart of the one manifesting faith. Giving oneself ourselves totally to another is a very dangerous endeavor. In doing so, we disempower ourselves and empower another. We are placing our total trust in someone other than ourselves. In certain circumstances this is not a harmful endeavor. There are masters among us in every aspect of life who possess the ability to help and guide us toward certain ends. If a man seeks a beautiful piece of furniture in his home and is not adept at woodworking, he will seek a master craftsman to create the furniture desired. However, a wise consumer will seek to investigate works already created by the master to be sure that his skill will produce the desired effect. Once convinced, the consumer places his faith in the hands of the master. Because of his willingness to investigate a wise choice has been made and his faith will most likely be rewarded. However, should another consumer seek the same results from someone who claims mastery and blindly invest in his services, there is the possibility that this consumer might be dissatisfied and disappointed. This simple analogy is easy to understand and can be applied to matters of soul.

If a soul is seeking enlightenment and is attempting to communicate with spirit, then it should be cautious from whom it seeks guidance. To blindly follow another who professes to have mastery of the world of spirit, who can connect it to the energy of God, is a dangerous path to travel. There exist many masters of the spiritual realm who are available to guide a soul toward enlightenment, and they are marvelous and wonderful beings. A soul who encounters such masters has much to learn from them, and many benefits will be bestowed upon the seeker who accepts guidance and follows their lead. However, there are many that profess mastery and convince the seeker to blindly follow their ways. This is a very dangerous situation, for the seeker may be guided toward destructive forces that will gravely affect his existence on earth and in the universe. There are, unfortunately, dark forces of energy, just as there are forces of *Light*. A soul should be extremely careful to remain outside the forces of *Darkness*, for once captured by this energy, it is difficult to escape it.

G: This sounds quite dire. I can see how blind faith can render one helpless and diminished in power. However, the mention of dark energy and being captive in its energy is frightening. How does one escape this energy once captured by it?

Haitukulu: One escapes by seeking the *Light*. It is not difficult if the soul becomes focused on accessing *Light*. However, *Darkness* is not quick to release the soul, although the universe demands that release be granted. *Darkness* does not always present itself in a harsh and demanding manner. It is very often seductive and uses its seductive power to prevent the soul from truly seeking the *Light*. It convinces the soul that moving toward the *Light* is much too rigorous and demanding. It attempts to convince the soul that the *Light* is only a myth that the weak will seek to follow. It holds the soul captive through the rational mind. There are many more ways in which the *Darkness* exerts its influence, and many ways to counter it through the influence of the *Light*.

However, the most basic principle is for the soul to harbor true desire to move toward the *Light* and to make wise choices as to who will guide them. One must learn to ignore the seductive promises of those who claim to have exclusive connections to the *Light*, who encourage it to believe that theirs is the only path toward enlightenment. The true teacher encourages the student to be independent; the false teacher insists on dependence. My advice to any soul who is seeking to free himself from the bondage of *Darkness* is to seek guidance from the spirit of the Creator and to discern insights through the heart and soul, not the rational mind. Of course the mind is a powerful tool, yet that's just what the mind is; a tool. It is a wonderful tool that can be used to render incredible results in all avenues of life. However, for any tool to be used effectively, the user must understand its principles and substance to maximize the results it is capable of delivering.

I have a feeling at this moment that your mind is requiring a more simple explanation than the one I have just delivered.

G: You are correct. I understand in a feeling kind of way what you have described. Would you please simplify this explanation just a bit?

Haitukulu: Certainly. Learn to have faith in the spirit of the Creator; learn to have faith in the perceptions of your soul. Trust your soul when you are seeking guidance, for your soul possesses true knowing. Learning the true workings of your soul requires personal introspection, thus the need for meditation and prayer. Know your prayers will be answered as they are meant to be. Trust only those in whom your soul feels comfort, and pray always for the presence of *Light*. Remember that the journey of each soul is individual and that all souls are a part of the energy of the Creator. Each of us is a part of all creation. Keep this in your soul, and you will keep it in your mind as we have discussed.

Have I simplified this concept enough for you to understand?

G: You certainly have, and I'm grateful to you for doing so. I do have a question regarding what you said about being a part of all of creation. Many of the entities that have come forward thus far have said the same thing, that we are all a part of creation. I'm beginning to believe this to be so and that by keeping in mind that whatever we do is for the good of all creation, we are helping to generate *Light* into the universe. I'm guessing that you will support this assumption.

Haitukulu: I do so most readily, for that is a universal principle, a universal truth. When we keep in mind that every thought, every action affects the universal energy, then it becomes easier to think and act in a correct manner. Of course we are all individual and unique in our existence.

You are asking, what is correct? There are so many energies in the universe, so many different frequencies of vibration. Our perceptions will not always be the same as the perceptions of others. Our needs, experiences, interests, and desires cannot possibly match those of all whom exist. Yet we must understand this so we will not judge others based on what we understand as correct. Correct means from the heart and soul, and for the good of all creation.

It is important to learn and practice principles of the universe. It is important to be aware of the forces of *Light* and *Darkness*. When this is understood, then the soul is capable of choosing the *Light*. All spirit is exposed to the duality of *Light* and *Darkness*. Actively choosing to dwell in the *Light* will move a soul toward the end of the spectrum of *Light*, thus expelling *Darkness* from its being. Understand that this is a process of development and often an arduous task. However, enlightenment is a wonderful journey and one each soul will seek at some point in its existence. Be wise in your journey. Perceive life from your soul. Avoid the seductions of *Darkness*. Seek masters of *Light*. These are principles that you now comprehend and principles that those reading this book may understand and employ if they so desire. There is a joy in love, and love is a true reason for existing. Love is God. Love is the ultimate gift.

G: You are so profound, Haitukulu. I wish that I could adequately convey to the reader just how kind and wonderful you are. You have been my ideal for so many years now. I often wonder if the communications I am receiving are merely my imagination or if they are real. Would you please comment on this?

Haitukulu: My friend, I understand your apprehension regarding all that you are experiencing. The perceptions you have developed are not of a worldly nature and thus are not easily validated. Consider what other entities have thus far explained to you regarding frequencies of vibration. You have learned to access a finer frequency than that which is common to the human consciousness, although all of life is capable of understanding this perception. It is not by chance that you have arrived at this particular station in life, it is a process in which you have partaken for quite some time. Reflect upon your journey, and you will understand the truth of this statement. Do not hide what you have learned. Rejoice in knowing that you are accessing energy that is the right of all souls. Also understand that this knowing does not make you either superior or inferior to other souls of the universe, it merely makes you who you are. Your endeavor to share your knowledge with others of your planet is commendable and truly important. Of course there are certain consequences of sharing ideas of a spiritual nature.

G: I think I might understand what the consequences are, but I would appreciate if you would state them.

Haitukulu: Of course. You must understand that those who do not care to consider them in any way will most certainly reject any enlightened ideas that are outside the realm of their belief system. Your ideas will be considered folly by many; you may be subject to ridicule. You might even experience the ire of those whose minds will regard your words as blasphemous. There always exists a danger when expressing ideas that are in opposition to the established ideals of others.

However, the consequences do not outweigh the rewards of expressing the faith that is yours. Your belief in the existence of the energy of love is shared by many, and it is those souls who are seeking to understand and validate this existence within themselves who will accept and appreciate the ideas you have brought forward. When anyone communicates love, then rewards will become manifest, for love is the truest of all energies that exist. Be fearless in your expression of universal truths.

Remember, we all exist as a part of the energy of the Creator. Every correct thought and action we execute exists for the highest good of all creation. As more souls contribute to the energy of love, the universe becomes strengthened in *Light*. Find your strength in the *Light*. Learn to receive as well as to give, for, in receiving, one's ability to give becomes more powerful. Seek guidance and understanding, and it will become manifest in your life. The way of spirit is natural to the soul. It is in the process of living that we may become distanced from the source of true inspiration, for a part of the process of living in the human condition is designed to challenge one's faith. Do not fret about this; merely understand the existence of the challenge. You are free to believe whatever you wish to believe. Your soul will know as much as you allow it to know. There is such simplicity in the truth and power of spirit, one must merely simplify life and allow the truth to become manifest. May all who read this statement understand it from the soul. It is my gift to you all.

G: Haitukulu, that was such a powerful insight, and stated so beautifully. I'm sensing that this interview is complete. Am I correct?

Haitukulu: Yes, my friend. I have stated all that is necessary at this time. Of course there is so much more to know, for learning is an infinite process. However, comprehension often functions best when done in small doses. Absorb all I have said and allow the message to bring peace to your being. Allow the understanding of love to open love's energy to you. As each soul manifests love, the universe grows stronger, one soul at a time. The truth is simple. Seek truth.

G: I truly wish that I could find the words appropriate to say to you. You have been such a wonderful teacher to me over the years, and my gratitude is immeasurable. In the *Light* of simplicity, I will merely say thank you. I know you will understand the power of those words. Your mastery is incredible; I will remain your student eternally.

In the spirit of this book, would you be kind enough to express a final word of wisdom to the reader?

Haitukulu: Of course. Learn to love, for in learning to love, you learn to truly live.

G: Thank you again for sharing your enlightened insights. Good day to you, Haitukulu.

Haitukulu: Good day to you, my friend. May you and all others have many, many more.

The Angel of Zarton

Soul as Creator

The Angel of Zarton is a most unique spirit. He is a very, very special spirit to me. I met him so many years ago, when I wrote my first story titled: "Toop Toope, Baby." I recall that at that time I was definitely frightened to meet him. He appeared as a deity who has been granted permission by the Creator Himself to create his own universe. The universe that he created is a most special one. In it exists seven planets, each with its own unique inhabitants. The Angel of Zarton dwells on the planet called Uversa, which is the central planet of his universe. I recall that I found him very frightening, for he was directly linked to the Creator and at that time I considered that to be most intimidating. Although I consciously knew that I was involved in a story, I still felt the power of his presence. He is not merely a character in a story; he is a true deity.

I recall the reverence I felt when he made his appearance in the Great Hall. He was so very regal in his appearance, and I must admit that I did not wish for him to cast his gaze upon me, for I felt quite unworthy of his attention. I realized that he possessed a benevolent nature, yet I felt unworthy of his benevolence. I imagined that he possessed a harsh and judgmental side to his being as well, much as I was led to believe about the Creator in my formative religious education. It amazes me that at this moment in time that he is actually coming forward to reveal his truths, and that through his revelations I no longer fear him. In fact, I feel very attracted to his energy and sense his true kindness and compassion for all beings of the universe.

I find it fascinating that he has created a universe of his own, having been given a special gift from the Creator Himself. It is through his act of creation that I have learned that I too possess the power of creation. In fact, each of us possesses this same power. What we choose to create is up to each one of us.

With this said, it is time to call upon the Angel of Zarton to come forward with his insights and revelation of truth. It is with respect and gratitude that this interview begins.

* * *

The Angel of Zarton

G: Welcome, it is a true pleasure to have this opportunity to speak with you.

Angel of Zarton: It is my pleasure to be speaking with you. I am happy that you have carried me in your consciousness for so many years. I am also happy that you have surrendered your fear of me. Although there was never a need for you to feel uncomfortable in my presence, it was necessary for your development to reach this understanding. I applaud your persistence and sincerely wish that you apply this knowledge to all aspects of your daily living as well as the development of your spirit and soul.

G: I truly understand your statement and appreciate your patience and benevolence. I am asking that you reveal insights regarding the process and power of creation.

Angel of Zarton: I'll begin by stating that every being in the universe possesses the power to create a universe of his or her own. However, the universe of which I speak is not of a physical sense. Some would have you believe that life at certain levels is merely an illusion. Life is eternal, and each moment of eternity is a part of a being's reality. Therefore the physical environment in which one dwells, the physical body that one possesses, are quite real at the moment of possession. There are things that can be done to modify one's environment, and even one's body. I'm certain that you can understand this concept. However, even though there are modifications that can be made, not all can be changed in the physical alone. Yes, one is capable of reshaping the body; one can alter a physical home. However, true change is internal. The true change is made manifest in the soul, through the world of spirit.

There is a way that one is capable of creating a personal universe. All beings of your planet create their own reality. Each individual ultimately perceives life in his and her own way. As an example, consider siblings raised in the same home and exposed to the same values. Although their physical environment is the same, their realities may be quite different. How they perceive life is their individual choice. Each will view life in his own way. Of course there might be many similarities in their belief and value systems, yet each will define life individually. Try to understand this concept and you will understand the process of creating your own universe.

G: You are making this sound quite simplistic. I'm sure creating your own universe cannot be such an easy task to accomplish. Please explain.

Angel of Zarton: Creating one's universe truly is a simple task. All one must do is understand the basic principles of the universe. Arriving at this understanding is the obstacle that many humans fail to overcome, for many do not perceive the obstacle itself.

G: What might that obstacle be?

Angel of Zarton: The obstacle is refusal to believe.

G: That is the obstacle, the refusal to believe? That sounds much too simple!

The Angel of Zarton

Angel of Zarton: Again, it is that simple. The reasons for lack of belief are complex in many ways, yet the obstacle itself is quite simple. Allow me to explain.

Belief is something that originates from one's inner knower, which is the soul. Being in touch with one's soul should be a simple endeavor, but unfortunately it often is not. There are many ways that one allows the soul's influence and voice to be ignored. The mind is the biggest culprit.

G: What do you mean, the mind is a culprit?

Angel of Zarton: Many societies promote the mind to be the largest influence in one's perceptions. One is constantly bombarded with stimuli in this direction. Those who dwell in capitalistic societies receive messages of this nature on a constant basis, both actively and subliminally. The mind becomes filled with thoughts about ways to "get ahead." People are encouraged to attain material possessions and are often led to believe that possessions equate to wealth. A cycle is created in which the mind becomes so active with materialism thought that the soul becomes neglected. The voice of the soul becomes ignored; thus the creative force of the universe lies dormant within. The voice of the active mind drowns out the voice of the soul.

G: I have witnessed, as well as experienced, what you have just described. It seems to take a lot of work to tune out the mind and tune into the soul.

Angel of Zarton: It does not take a lot of work. It merely requires attention. It is a matter of perception.

G: I've come to realize this concept. Perhaps you will elaborate on this.

Angel of Zarton: With pleasure. As you know, the entire universe is made of energy. Energy exists at all levels and manifests itself through vibrations. Thus, life forms of similar vibrations are visible to one another. However, simply because all forms of energy are not visible does not mean they do not exist.

The human mind was created as a tool of the soul. It is the "seer" of the spirit, the mechanism the soul uses for survival in its physical form. It is the human body that houses the soul. And it is the soul that is the essence of all beings, for each soul is a unique part of the Creator. The Creator is the life force of energy for all of creation.

The Creator's energy is the energy of Love, the purest of all energy that exists. All beings possess this spirit, yet not all beings manifest it. Love exists always, in all dimensions. It will not seek you; it is you who must seek Love. Keep in mind that the vibrations of Love are often subtle and seekers must be both patient and vigilant in their journeys toward Love. I am using the term Love, but it is synonymous with the Creator.

G: That sounds rather simple. So why is it often so difficult to understand soul as a simple concept?

The Angel of Zarton

Angel of Zarton: That is for you to answer. The journey toward Love is an individual one. Your thoughts, perceptions, feelings about Love are yours alone. This is how you create your own universe. You create your own universe because your universe consists of your individual perceptions. Wherever you live, work, or travel your reality belongs to you.

G: It seems that some people have accessed this creative power. They know so much about it. Should we follow someone who knows these secrets?

Angel of Zarton: You have asked that question on behalf of those who are faced with that decision. It is kind of you to do so!

Listen carefully, my young friend. There are no secrets, there truly are not. Of course there are mystical happenings, but they are not secrets. The enlightened ones are merely accessing vibrations of frequencies differently from those who exist in the human form. All beings possess the capability to attune their vibrations to other frequencies. It is not difficult. It certainly does take some practice, it requires attention, but there is no rush. Life is eternal and exists in different forms. Relax in the energy that you are experiencing. Understand Love from your personal perspective, your personal energy.

G: I do not intend to appear irreverent, but you did not really respond to my question about following others.

Angel of Zarton: Forgive me if I appeared to be misdirected. Your question is important, and I will address it. There are many masters who exist, many masters who can guide you in the direction of enlightenment. What you must do is listen to the masters with an open mind and open heart. Absorb what feels right to you. Receive whatever energy your being is longing to receive. But do not cling to every word you hear; do not allow anyone's mind to become your mind. Borrow whatever ideas and energy that fortify the knower inside of you. Use what you have borrowed to shape your individual reality, your personal connection to the energy of the Creator. In doing so you become the creator of your own universe. Create from your heart; create from your inner knower. Create from your soul.

I am offering some powerful advice. Listen carefully to those who teach, but do not judge them. Do not empower them by surrendering your self completely to them. Do not totally submit your being to anyone but the Creator. Learn from masters, but be careful to maintain your individual *Light*, your individual soul. Each soul, including yours, is an integral part of the whole of creation. Each soul is a powerful part of the great energy of the Creator.

Another thought to consider is to be careful not to condemn another whose message is in opposition to your personal beliefs. There are many vibrations, many frequencies that exist in the universe. Your task is to discover what frequency leads you to Love. Yours is correct for you, so strive to understand your own energy. Follow your individual path toward Love. Judge no one, for in judging others you are distracting yourself from Love.

The Angel of Zarton

G: That is a beautiful concept. I thank you for your explanation.

Angel of Zarton: It is my pleasure to share with you. Hopefully you will share with others. Sharing is critical to the energy of Love. Do not speak to others with authority, speak to others with compassion. Speak from your soul; think from your soul. Do not be frustrated if others do not share your perspective. Do not feel defeated if you do not understand what others say to you. Each of us is a part of the whole of creation; each of us is a part of Love. We participate in Love however we choose.

It is no one's place to criticize those who seem to miss the true understanding of existence, which is simply generating the spirit and energy of Love. See each soul as a part of all of creation, each soul as a part of the energy of Love.

G: There are so many mean-spirited people in the world, people who will harm you. What about them?

Angel of Zarton: There will always be those who exist very far from Love. It is wise to keep yourself distanced from that energy if it makes you uncomfortable. However, you can exist close to such beings and not be affected by their energy. Who you align yourself with is up to you. You may, through circumstances, be aligned with others who are distant from Love. You may be forced to share your space, but you are not forced to yourself. Your mind and soul belong only to you. This is another perception to remind you that you are a creator of your own universe.

G: I understand what you have said. We are often cast into situations that align us with negative people. They might be coworkers, neighbors, relatives, and any number of people. They might even be criminals who randomly impose themselves upon us. I ask this reverently, but would you please offer an insight regarding this matter?

Angel of Zarton: Of course I will. It is a difficult concept for many to accept, but life is not random. All interactions occur for the specific purpose of strengthening the spirit. One calls energy toward them, even if that soul is not aware of doing so. One should come to understand that thoughts consist of energy. This energy is "broadcast", so to speak, into the infinite field of energy. There exists the universal principle that like attracts like. Thus fearful thoughts will attract fearful circumstances. In this same knowing, loving thoughts will attract Love. In every interaction there is a lesson for the soul. It is the purpose of life on earth; it is the nature of the dimension. I understand that this concept might be difficult to rationalize, but there are certain truths in the universe that exist. Acceptance of truth can be accomplished by perceiving life through the soul, through one's inner knower. The more influence the material mind exerts on an individual, the greater the difficulty of attaining the true understanding of Love.

Thinking through the soul requires surrender; it requires faith. The faith to which I refer is not a blind faith, a submission to the message others would have you believe. It is a surrender to the inner knower of your being, that part of each soul that needs no explanation. That part of you is the Creator, and all beings of creation share it as one. We are all connected

The Angel of Zarton

to the whole. Understanding this connection is critical to one's enlightenment. Once understood, a new level of consciousness is revealed, and in this consciousness one becomes truly empowered. In this consciousness one learns to create. And in creating one participates in the great energy of the Creator. You become the Creator along with the Creator.

G: This is an amazing insight! I truly understand! I wish that I could be of that mindset in all moments. Life sometimes distracts me from that energy. How can this be prevented, this slipping away from the Creator?

Angel of Zarton: That is for you to answer. What is of foremost importance is that once you recognize the energy of Love, you do whatever it takes to maintain it. Each soul has its own method of doing so. Once the taste of the Creator fills your soul, you will long to continue experiencing it. However, it requires conscious effort. All things in life that one seeks to maintain require a conscious effort to do so. Speak with an artist, a musician, and an athlete. Speak with any of the people who are dwelling in an energy they desire to maintain, and they will tell you it is so. Yet if that energy fulfills you, you do not struggle to maintain it. Maintenance is not considered "work." Moments of difficulty do occur, but they are moved through and passed by one's passion. The same is true in regard to maintaining a consciousness of Love's energy. Love's energy is the greatest of all energies that exist. Being a conscious part of this energy will hold your attention. So, even if you feel separated from Love, if you hold its power in your heart, you will not be separated at all.

Life on earth requires attention, and energy must be spent in many ways. When life requires you to deal with it, you must do so to survive. However, while dealing with whatever life either offers or imposes on you, do so with this knowing that you are part of Love—you are part of the Creator's energy. All of creation is, no matter where one exists in the universe.

G: I understand that we truly are all a part of the Creator. How we know, perceive, and understand the Creator is an individual concept, a conscious choice. In knowing the Creator we choose what we create. Am I correct in this concept?

Angel of Zarton: You are more than correct—you are wise. We create ourselves every moment of every day. All beings of existence do so. We can create from so many perspectives, from so many energies! We have a choice from where we choose to create. Never labor under the misconception that you are not creative. Never. One does not need to be an expert in art forms to be creative. All one must do is simply be. Simply be yourself. Of course one can create havoc and turmoil as well as peace and beauty; one must understand this at all moments in time. Unfortunately there are many who do just that. There are numerous individuals who create negative and destructive circumstances rather than creating *Love*. With this understanding it becomes important to seek the source of the true power of creative energy. It is important to seek the creative power of Love.

As you seek this power, you draw it toward you. The energy of Love will enter you when you desire it. And once it enters, you will know and understand its presence. It is when you become one with this energy that your true creative power will fully manifest itself. It is from this source that miracles are created. It is from this source that lust for personal power becomes diminished and finally extinguished. It is from this source that one becomes selfless. And in becoming selfless one discovers his true self.

Wisdom is highly revered in the world of spirit, for in wisdom is born the tools to generate *Light*. And in generating *Light* one is living Love. I could elaborate this insight in simple terms, but I will not do so, for those who truly seek Love must absorb the concept in their own time, in their own way. But the words will touch a place in the souls seeking to be enlightened, and the understanding they desire through their individual spirit will be their interpretive device. It is then that the power of creativity will become truly understood.

G: Your insights are so powerful! You have opened my eyes to the true power of creativity. My gratitude is immense! Do you have any more insights to share?

Angel of Zarton: There is one of great importance. Align yourself with masters. Learn from those who truly understand.

G: How do we find and recognize masters?

Angel of Zarton: You invite them into your life through prayer, and you recognize them through your soul—your inner knower. It is a very simple thing to do.

Masters are around you everywhere, in all of life, in all of creation. The earth is filled with masters. Look to any means of existence, and you will find them. However, exercise caution when seeking teachers. There are many that would have you believe that they are true masters. There are many that are eager to empower themselves by accepting your surrender. You must be cautious with whom you seek guidance.

G: I think I already know the answer to how we recognize masters!

Angel of Zarton: Of course you do—it is with your inner knower. This is why it is vital that you learn to recognize that part of your spirit. It is essential to be in touch with your soul if you are to realize your true power to create. Know your inner knower!

G: I understand. But I do have another question. Can we learn from those who are not masterful?

Angel of Zarton: Again, my response is that of course you can. You can and do learn from everyone around you. However, in matters that are of true importance to your journey, it is best to devote your learning energy to those who can teach you best.

But do not ignore anyone who offers you insights that will assist you on your path toward enlightenment. There are lessons to learn from everyone who crosses your path. Learn from each interaction you have with others. Simple interactions bear valuable lessons that will appear to you when you learn to view the world as a place that is filled with all of creation. You can also learn from the thoughts and actions of those whose thoughts and actions violate the values of your soul. By turning away from such persons, you learn to turn toward your true self. However, do not judge those who differ from yourself. Judge no one; not even those who pass judgment on you.

I would like to continue my reference to learning from masters. Understand that there are lessons the soul yearns to comprehend and absorb, for the soul seeks true enlightenment. While searching, the soul will encounter numerous energies, and the lessons most ardently sought will capture the seeker's attention and energy. When you, or any seeker, place your attention within a particular energy, it is wise to journey in the presence of masters. There are earthly lessons to be learned, as well as those of pure spirit.

A simple analogy would be this: you are desirous to learn to play a musical instrument. You know very little about playing and seek a teacher. Who will teach you best? It will be someone of mastery. Of course you should understand that there are many levels of mastery within the same energy and as you become more proficient in your own skills and perceptions you will seek those of more accomplished levels than your own. You will likely arrive at a point in your seeking when you will be included in mastery and you will be given the opportunity to help others along their way. Seek to learn from those who teach you best, for you in turn will be able to teach others well, thus perpetuating *Light* into the universe.

You will recognize masters by your inner knower, your feeling from deep within you. Do not hesitate to move away from those who will not teach you well. And do not lament when the time arrives to move away from those who teach with greatness. The journey toward enlightenment is continuous, and one must understand this concept to avoid stagnation. You may dwell in a wonderful energy with a wonderful master for a sustained period of time. However, the universe is structured so that nothing lasts forever. The only energy that lasts forever is the energy of Love, yet that too contains infinite energies within it. Move always in the energy of Love, and keep your spirit open to masters who will assist you along your path toward enlightenment.

Be patient; be vigilant in your desire to attain this understanding, this knowing from within. Look past the distractions of life, past the periods of seeming separation from the energy of Love. Hold fast to your desire to be one with all of creation. By doing so you become creation itself, and thus a true creator.

I understand that this explanation might be a bit abstract, but it is offered as a seed of insight. Invite the desire to be one with the creative energy into your heart. True desire is the seed of creation. Plant it within you, nourish it with kindness and respect, and be patient as it germinates, then blossoms within you. Your journey is unique, different from that of all other souls. Yet the destination is the same as all souls who seek enlightenment. It is to be one with the Creator, who truly is Love.

G: You've made it so clear, Angel; I thank you so much for all you've shared. You are such a kind and wise entity. I am grateful to you for bestowing your energy upon me, as well as on those who will read this on their journey toward enlightenment.

The Angel of Zarton

My spirit is filled with true gratitude. Would you please offer a parting insight?

Angel of Zarton: I do so with great pleasure. Relax in life, even in moments of turmoil. You create yourself in every breath that you take, from your first until your last. In creating yourself, you create your universe, your inner world of spirit. Live and think through your spirit, be in touch at all moments with your inner knower. Allow your soul to guide your mind, and you will understand the power of creation. Open your heart, and your mind will follow.

G: Thank you once again for all that you are. I'm so happy for your patience. I see you so differently than I did on our first encounter! I wish you peace, and I promise to share your insights. You are simply wonderful!

Angel of Zarton: Your kind words touch me. Go in peace and in the energy of Love, my friend. Fill your heart and soul with joy!

G: I will, Angel of Zarton. I most certainly will!

Anisha

Soul Mates and Twin Flames

Anisha is a female spirit whom I met some time ago. I enjoy her company because her spirit is so light and lively. She is filled with smiles that radiate a true understanding of love. She speaks with me about matters of the heart, for her essence is the true heart of love. It is from Anisha that I receive insights into relationships among people. She has spoken to me before regarding how souls unite and share.

I have often closed my eyes and seen myself sitting high upon a hill that overlooks a beautiful lake with Anisha sitting beside me. With my eyes closed, I am able to see her form. I am able to experience her spirit. I am also able to hear the sounds of nature. With my eyes closed, I can see so many things!

Anisha's voice is airy and filled with gentle laughter. Her spirit is filled with wisdom and understanding, and she knows much about the gentle spirit of creation. It is with true delight that I invite her to speak with you.

* * *

Anisha

G: Welcome, Anisha. I am writing with a warm and wide smile on my face! You bring such happiness with your spirit. It is a treat to have you share your insights with all who are endeavoring to read this book. I'm certain they will enjoy your company!

Anisha: Thank you so much! Your kind words move me to smile brightly. It is *you* who is making *me* smile!

G: This is a happy interview! But I think that we should get started, if you don't mind. We must share this happiness with others. Please tell us what you wish to share.

Anisha: Certainly. I wish to discuss how souls relate to each other, how spirits are shared.

G: Are you referring to soul mates?

Anisha: Yes, I am. But I am referring to more than soul mates. I'm here to explain about the value of all relationships that one encounters in life. Also, I wish to discuss the issue of a twin flame, the true completion of your soul.

G: That sounds very interesting and uplifting. I'm going to enjoy hearing your insights.

Anisha: Thank you. You should enjoy our conversation because it's really about love. Each soul houses at least a spark of love within it. Love feels good, and it's fun if you allow it to be.

G: May we begin with the concept of soul mates? It seems that many people have that on their minds.

Anisha: Sure! We'll begin with soul mates. What specifically would you like to know?

G: Do they really exist?

Anisha: Of course they do! Soul mates abound on earth, and in all realms of the universe as well. Soul mates are everywhere! I know you will ask me what truly constitutes a soul mate. Am I correct in this assumption?

G: Yes, you are. How did you know that?

Anisha: The female character of one's soul has a powerful intuition regarding matters of love! With that said I will begin.

A soul mate is someone who touches your soul, who understands your energy; whose energy you understand as well. A soul mate is someone who feels right to you in some way. He or she might be very much like you in thoughts, feelings, taste. He or she might be the opposite of you as well. But a soul mate will share your energy and enrich your life in some way. A soul mate may bring you pure joy or may create turmoil in your life. Yet a soul mate will always help you along your journey.

G: That certainly is a different concept to understand! I can appreciate the idea that a soul mate will help one as he or she journeys, but the concept of creating turmoil is one I need explained to me!

Anisha: No, you don't. You already know what I mean by that. You are feigning surprise so that those who are reading this and do not understand the concept will find comfort in their confusion. This is generous of you!

G: I can't fool you!

Anisha: No, you cannot. So do not even try! Now, where were we?

G: You were explaining how soul mates help one's life, even by causing turmoil.

Anisha: Yes, it's true. That happens often. All souls in the universe are moving toward enlightenment. It's the natural state of the soul, the true essence of existence. Some do so consciously, while others seem totally unaware. The universe is made up of all of creation, and each individual is truly a spiritual being. Understanding this, one can grasp the concept that none of us is alone. We are all a part of the same great energy.

Moving toward enlightenment is the ultimate goal. However, there are so many paths to take, so many possibilities! Each path is in reality a stream of energy, and most streams are inhabited by many souls of like or similar vibration. It is in every stream of energy that one encounters soul mates, who are souls journeying in the same great energy, souls who are in essence journeying together.

G: Excuse me for interrupting, but a thought suddenly arose in my consciousness. If this is true, we may encounter many different soul mates during the course of the journey!

Anisha: Of course—that is a simple truth. One can encounter many, many soul mates during the course of a lifetime. So too it might be the opposite. One might encounter a few or even just one soul mate during the course of a lifetime. It's all a matter of which stream of energy one chooses to travel.

G: Do we choose our stream of energy, or are we placed in it?

Anisha: You choose your stream of energy. One might not be conscious of doing so, but it is a choice. There are influences that are external. One's environment has much to do with how the conscious mind perceives life. Survival is the human's greatest instinct. It shapes one's perceptions. One who lives in a war-torn country must rely on a heightened awareness of survival skills. One living in peace, comfort, and safety will not sense survival instincts with the same intensity. But all humans are operating on survival instincts; they are inherent in each person.

G: I understand your insight, but am a bit confused as to how this relates to soul mates.

Anisha: You can't fool me! Thank you for keeping me focused! Sometimes I ramble a bit; it's just my nature!

The point I'm trying to convey is this. No matter what condition in life one experiences, there is inherent in all souls the desire to become enlightened. Some feel it more than others do but, as I've already explained, all souls harbor the desire. That is where the stream of energy becomes manifest. Other spirits before me have explained the concept of frequencies of vibration. Vibrations are real and contain different frequencies, different densities. As one becomes more aware of spirit, then the vibration becomes less dense, it becomes finer. Those who experience finer vibrations are more able to recognize those of similar vibrations on a conscious level. Those who are vibrating at a more dense frequency do not recognize others in the same way. Recognition becomes more subliminal, often just a feeling. Yet all souls seek to align themselves with others of like vibrations.

Your mind is filling with compassion for those who might consider this pure rubbish, am I correct?

G: Here we go again! That's exactly what I'm thinking!

Anisha: You certainly are a difficult one! You are making me smile! You also need to hear how a negative interaction can indicate a soul mate.

G: You're doing it again!

Anisha: I will address the matter of negative relations first, then move toward the positive. Will that place you more at ease?

G: Yes, it will. Thank you.

Anisha: All right, I will begin. I've already stated that soul mates accompany each other on the path toward enlightenment. This is a simple concept to understand. Even the isolate will experience the process of a soul mate. It might be as a casual relationship, but every soul experiences a spark of knowing. It is important to understand, though, that not all souls will respond to a soul mate. There are souls who are so wrought with negative energy that they can accept love and understanding from no one. Love and understanding are always available, yet the individual rejects them for whatever reasons he or she chooses. It is not your or my place to judge them, or even to speculate as to why one rejects love. It simply happens, and only that individual is capable of knowing why it is so. This knowing is contained within their spirit. Yet if that soul, or any soul, chooses to move toward the positive, to place itself in a different energy, it is free to do so. And in doing so it will encounter others who are sharing a similar energy.

Allow me to offer a very concrete and simple example. A person may suddenly discover that he has an unhealthy condition in his body, possibly one of which he never even knew existed. His focus in thinking suddenly changes. He becomes aware of this malady, sometimes to the point of total consumption of conscious thought. He reads about the condition, speaks to others about it. What usually happens is he finds others who share a similar condition, or who have at least heard of it. Then an unusual phenomenon often develops. He seems to run across more and more people who share their concern and people of this mindset often become familiar with each other. They begin to share the energy in which they are traveling. They might support and encourage each other, offering comfort and understanding. In this shared energy they are sharing their souls, thus becoming soul mates.

The same is true for those who are actively seeking enlightenment. In a soul's journey toward enlightenment, he or she will encounter others of a similar vibration, others of a similar mindset, and relationships are shared. And remember this: a relationship does not need to be deep and intimate, although that does often happen. But those traveling in a similar stream of energy will appear and help one another along the journey. I think if you take a moment to think about this, you will understand the merit of my explanation. Take a moment to reflect on all the energies you have experienced during your tenure on earth and those who have appeared while you were in a particular energy. Go ahead, you'll see!

G: That is quite an amazing insight. In a moment's reflection, I can truly see! Thanks, Anisha! I have been in many different energies and have shared them with so many others. You speak the truth!

Now, I do have another question to ask at this moment. You mentioned that soul mates might sometimes cause turmoil in our lives. What is that about?

Anisha: This is a good question to ask at this moment. Let's deal with the uncomfortable truth first so we can end up with happy thoughts. I prefer to exist in a pleasant stream of consciousness.

Other spirits have mentioned that all interactions serve a purpose on the path toward enlightenment; that is not a difficult concept to understand. However, sometimes a soul mate will find another while he or she is journeying in a particular stream of energy, when one is struggling to understand his or her being. When first joined in spirit the relationship feels right, it is a wonderful experience. However, the energy that is being shared might dissipate, leaving each seeker in a different mindset, a different perception. Some souls recognize this shift in energy and move on, grateful for the time spent together and lessons learned. There will always remain a connection in their souls, and a strong feeling will prevail inside of each soul forever. I'm sure you can understand this; it's happened to you in your lifetime.

However, not all relationships are resolved in that manner. Many times when energies shift between soul mates, a great turmoil arises and endings are bitter. This occurs because one partner—or both partners—fails to recognize that their journeys are leading them in different directions, that they are being called to travel along different paths. Souls existing without a conscious understanding of enlightenment often experience this tumultuous ending. Worse still, many continue to remain together, existing in entirely different energies, thus causing frustration. Living in constant frustration often promotes anger, which clouds one's perception and can lead to hostile and sometimes violent behavior. The earth is filled with stories that validate this.

Yet another scenario occurs when one soul mate is perfectly happy in a shared energy while the other has felt a pull to move toward another direction. This too leads to tremendous turmoil and those of more dense vibrations are not likely to handle things very well. In all separation of soul lies a potential for hatred and violence. Yet in all separation also lies the potential to truly understand the process of the journey toward enlightenment and the role of the soul mate in helping one in this journey. There is no well-defined rule that exists regarding how a soul handles shifts in energy. All circumstances are unique and depend upon the vibration of the individuals involved. Understanding this will help one to understand that our journeys are individual experiences and the more we understand about the realm of spirit, the greater we can deal with energies in which we choose to travel.

Yet the turmoil itself, the upsetting of one's very being, creates a unique opportunity for the individual soul to understand so much about itself! It sees its strength or weakness. It discovers its capacity for compassion and understanding. It forces one to look their existence straight in the eye and make decisions as to how one will proceed. You can understand the many, many different ways one will perceive the turmoil, how some will embrace it while others shrink from it. But the point is, the turmoil will jar the soul into seeking on some level, and it is in the process of seeking that one attains at least a feeling of spirit. So in reality, souls that cause turmoil are actually helping one another. I understand that many reading this will find it difficult to absorb, but once understood beyond the ego then it becomes quite simple to comprehend.

I don't wish to dwell in this mindset, if you don't mind, G. There are simply too many scenarios regarding separation of energy among soul mates. Souls like themselves appear in the journey toward enlightenment. Try to understand that energy shifts from time to time. Within this concept one will be able to understand the difficulty he or she might be experiencing. If one is troubled, turn toward the Creator for explanations that will clarify issues of unrest. In the Creator, the answers are found. Each soul experiences the Creator in his or her own special way. Just keep in mind that soul mates will appear at many moments in one's journey, and a soul mate does not appear by chance. Be grateful to the soul that travels with you, even if the relationship is tumultuous. A point in one's journey will arrive when one will recognize a soul mate's purpose and significance to him or her, and will be grateful for the insights gleaned in a relationship.

G: Thank you for that explanation, Anisha. I could sense that your energy had diminished a bit toward the completion of that insight. You completed it, though, because it is important to you that those who are experiencing heartache at the hand of another might be comforted. That is an act of love.

Anisha: Yes, it is an act of love. To be honest, I love love! With the heavy side of soul mates addressed, it is time to move toward the positive. Are you ready to smile?

G: Sure am!

Anisha: Good, then let's smile for a while. That's what I do best! Now, let's discuss the lighter side of soul mates. How they help each other experience insights that produce joy!

G: You have my attention. Let's go!

Anisha: Isn't smiling fun? Isn't a smiling heart easier to enjoy than a heavy one? You do not have to answer. I know you understand!

Now, I'd like to speak of how soul mates have a positive effect on each other, how they bring each other joy!

Many labor under the notion that a soul mate is a once-in-a-lifetime partner who enters your life and remains with you forever. That is a half-truth, actually. There are many soul mates who may enter your life, at many different points in the journey. There are numerous levels on which souls share. Some are sharing thoughts and experiences, while others share on a very close and intimate level. They may remain with you or continue on another path. But the fact is, and this is a fact, that even if a soul mate steps onto a path that leads in another direction, he or she will remain within your soul forever. Once someone touches your soul and you recognize the interaction, that person remains within you for eternity.

Recognizing a soul mate is not difficult to do if you open your mind to the concept that a soul mate needn't be a lover, a spouse, or a romantic companion. Those who think in those terms only might fail to recognize soul mates that enter their energy. A soul mate is simply a soul who enters your soul. To recognize a soul mate doesn't require thinking—it requires feeling. That's simply all there is to it!

G: That does sound quite simple. I guess most of us are guilty of trying way too hard to understand the world of spirit!

Anisha: That is so true! Spirit is revealed most easily when one is relaxed. Many who meditate understand this. But I don't wish to elaborate on methods of accessing spirit. Others have already done so. I wish to continue speaking of love. It's my essence, you know!

G: Please do! You are so light and refreshing. I enjoy your company so much!

Anisha: The feeling is quite mutual! Now, I've become sidetracked again! Where were we?

G: You were discussing how we might recognize soul mates, and that we might have many appear to us in our lifetime.

Anisha: Oh yes! That's so true! There can be many. Our souls are vast as the universe! Our heart and soul can hold an infinite amount of love if we allow them to. And love comes in many varieties, many flavors! It is the true essence of every soul that exists!

G: There is something that is confusing me at this moment. I can rationalize the concept that we might encounter many soul mates throughout the course of a lifetime. I truly can. I can understand how soul mates appear to somehow assist us along the journey. But what about the commitment of souls in relationships? Can you have more than one soul mate at a

Anisha

time? Can you love more than one partner? That's a difficult concept and a difficult question!

Anisha: Indeed it is, but it is a legitimate question and will require a lengthy explanation!

Even though many societies teach us that once a mate is chosen then all other intimate relations are to cease, it is really not the way things work in the universe. The universe thrives on love! Why should love be stifled when love hears the call? However, there are priorities that are important to uphold and adhere to in matters of soul. I'm not condoning the impulsive behavior to act upon one's desires. This is altogether different. Issues of morality are important and must be respected if it is an important part of one's life. Each soul understands its internal moral code.

Desire is a powerful force within the human psyche. Although many religions teach one to suppress desire, it often rages in a private part of the human mind. The mind is the power source of desires, not the heart. Many do not understand this concept. The mind releases chemicals into the body that are very powerful in their potential. There will be many souls reading this right now who can relate to this and might be under the influence of desire in their present moment.

It is most important to understand the nature of desire. Desire is an energy, one that builds up within one's body and produces a chemistry that causes a frenzy of energy to course through it. Desire often overpowers the mind and courses through the entire body, looking for a way to be released. The sex organs of humans is located in the second chakra, and for release to be achieved, the energy must pass through five other energy centers. However, desire is often repressed for many reasons. For some it might be because it is perceived as inappropriate behavior, for others a distraction from the energy of God. Still others view desire as much too consuming and shift their thoughts to safer places. But one must understand the basic principle. Repressed desire is exactly that. It is something repressed, not released. It will manifest itself in some way, for it is an energy that has been accessed. And it will be released in some way. How it becomes released is a completely individual choice!

G: Anisha, you seem to be getting sidetracked once more. You were addressing the issue of soul mates and have suddenly delved into issues of desire!

Anisha: I understand your concern. I am not sidetracked. There is a point to my discussion of desire.

G: Your mood suddenly sounds serious!

Anisha: It is, so please allow me to continue! Now, where was I?

G: You were addressing desire, how it is ultimately released.

Anisha: Oh yes, I remember. The truth is desire will be released, but it gets released in many ways. It is best to learn to transmute it through positive channels. Individuals who deem desire as inappropriate will often release it through immersing themselves in work or perhaps physical exercise. Or perhaps they might choose a creative endeavor. Everyone has his or her own method of release. Those who release desire in this way are ultimately being kind to themselves, for their release is positive and often productive.

Some souls that need to release desire might seek private methods of this release in a sexual way. Attitudes about sex differ throughout the world, and this release can be considered either healthy or inappropriate. Perception of such release is really an individual's own affair. I will say that if release in this fashion creates anxiety and guilt, then it is not appropriate and perhaps the mind might be trained to find an alternative method of release. Yet if it feels natural and right, then it is! I am not attempting to offend those whose religious values might be violated by this concept; I am merely stating a concept that must be considered through the soul, not the mind. The soul recognizes its own truth.

Some desires arise when one just wishes to feel the energy of another, simply to be comforted by the presence of a soul mate. By sharing this presence, the soul finds fulfillment and continues on its journey toward enlightenment with a joyful spirit. The presence of soul mates in one's life can be such an uplifting experience! It can create such an awesome love!

G: That sounds wonderful. I have experienced this a number of times in my lifetime. It is also safe to assume that soul mates may be of the same gender.

Anisha: Of course they are! Why does the male psyche equate love to sexual ideals? You do, you know!

G: Can't you stop reading my mind!

Anisha: No, I cannot. And I will not! Now listen carefully. I've mentioned before that soul mates are those souls who share energy with us and assist us on our journey toward enlightenment. If such a powerful phenomenon exists, then how could it possibly be limited to members of the opposite sex? It cannot be so. It is not difficult to understand that members of the same sex can be soul mates. Love is simply love. Romantic love is one aspect of love, but only one. Love comes in an infinite amount of expressions. And soul mates can be present in each one. I'm sure this is easy to understand.

G: It is, Anisha. I do understand. Soul mates exist on many levels, and some share more intimately with us than others do. Yet all those who enter our soul, who assist us on our journey, are soul mates. I guess you might say they are teammates on our journey of the soul!

Anisha: Very good, G! You've stated a very clever analogy. Good for you!

G: Thanks, Anisha! Now, you had mentioned at the very beginning of this interview the concept of twin flames. Would you address that one now?

Anisha: Ah, you saved the best for last. Very clever of you!

G: I have a good teacher!

Anisha

Anisha: I'll accept that as a compliment. Thank you! A twin flame is something very special, sacred actually! For a twin flame is the completion of one's soul. All souls have one, it is the natural way of the universe.

To understand the concept of a twin flame, look toward the universe itself. The universe exists because it has balance. A basic principle exists in physics. This principle states that for every action there is an equal and opposite reaction. This is how energy remains balanced. Think in simple terms of how this applies to life on earth. Night and day exist, as so light and dark. One sleeps so that he has energy when he is awake. The earth has a definite polarity, north and south. The body inhales and exhales. I am making the analogies quite basic, and I'm sure you could create many, many more if you care to. But the basic premise exists. For every action there is an equal and opposite reaction. With this being understood, consider that the soul has not one, but two parts that create itself. The completion of the soul is the soul's twin flame. That part is relatively easy to understand.

G: It is, but I sense it is something deeper. I also sense this excites you.

Anisha: Oh yes, it does! It excites me so! You see, the soul is both male and female. By itself it is incomplete. Coupled with its twin, it becomes one. Look to the species of your planet. Mating is necessary to perpetuate the continuum of life. It is the natural order of the universe. Of course cultures and different species vary greatly in behaviors once seeds are fertilized, yet for all life to continue, a form of completion must be experienced.

Try to understand this concept, then to elevate your consciousness to the highest form of all existence, the existence of the soul in the energy of the Creator, the energy of love. When a soul finds completion in this regard, then it is whole.

G: Whew! That's a bit difficult for me to understand completely. I think of myself as a total individual in one way, yet connected to all of creation in another. I have not really considered that I have a part of myself somewhere that completes me.

Anisha: Why have you not considered this?

G: I suppose because it's never really been brought to my attention. I really need a little help with this one, Anisha. Until now I've completely understood all you've said and asked questions on behalf of those who might need things explained more clearly. But in this moment, I am seeking a true understanding of what you are describing. Can you help me?

Anisha: This is true love, you know! You possess enough love to hunger for more!

Now listen to me carefully. Keep in mind the concepts of opposite polarity and balance. Keep in mind the fundamental need of union in order to perpetuate life. If you live alone, you will die alone. Yes, one can live alone and pass on many valuable lessons. That person's legacy can be rich. However, this soul will not be complete and will continue to seek completion in whatever energy it enters once the tenure on earth ceases.

There will arrive a moment in the journey when completion will exist. Even if you cannot visualize this, at least try to understand the concept. When completion occurs then the whole soul will bask in enlightenment. The soul may remain in this state or may choose to separate and journey alone. It is an individual choice and one that is made consciously.

G: That is an amazing concept. I need some time to absorb this!

Anisha: Take your time, G. You and all souls have forever to do so. What's your hurry?

G: I suppose I am feeling a need to truly understand a concept that is a bit foreign to me. I can grasp the concept that a soul has two parts and can become one—I can understand the theory of it. But I'm very confused as to why a soul that experiences completion might separate itself and journey on alone. Could you please explain that to me?

Anisha: Of course I will. I knew you would ask that question!

You see, the universe is eternal. Time is not measured as you understand it on earth. Souls continue to evolve in all moments. Even an enlightened soul continues to evolve, it is the natural order of the universe. As a soul evolves, it might seek enlightenment on different levels, thus the separation. The twins may gravitate toward a similar frequency or one of a different vibration. They will reunite once the lessons being sought are learned. It will take place in a moment that is meant to be.

I understand this is a concept quite foreign to your accepted belief. It might take you a while to comprehend, or you might reject it completely. Yet a twin flame does exist for each soul in all of creation. It is the way of the universe.

G: Assuming that this is a truth, I have two questions to ask. The first is, can a completed soul live on earth and understand its completion? The second is, how do we recognize a twin flame? How might the twin flame differ from a soul mate?

Anisha: Those are wonderful questions, and I'm glad that you asked them!

The first question is quite simple to answer. Of course a soul can be completed on earth and understand its completion, that is such a simple concept. Many, many souls exit it this way! Many souls spend multiple incarnations living this way. A completed soul is treasured in the universe, for a completed soul shines a *Light* that is necessary in maintaining the balance of energy in the universe. It has previously been stated that universal energy consists of both *Light* and *Darkness*. There are souls existing in both energies. The universe requires *Light*, and those souls who perceive this actually have an obligation to perpetuate *Light* on a conscious level. Many twin flames remain united not only for themselves, but also for the good of all creation. They attain a unified understanding of their obligation and use their strength to generate *Light*. It is not an existence merely for the self; it is an existence for the good of all of the Creator's energy!

I must tell you that those souls who decide to live in this manner, sharing their *Light* for the good of all of creation, are needed very badly in the earth's present energy! The balance of *Light* and *Darkness* is threatened in the present moment of earth's existence. A dark consciousness is spreading across the earth, and people in all regions of the world are feeling it. Dark energy is dangerous if it is not balanced by the energy of *Light*. It is crucial for all souls who understand *Light* to step beyond their individual selves and generate this *Light* into the universe. How they choose to do so is the individual choice of each soul, yet it is a necessary task. That is why twin flames who know each other should choose to remain united in this present moment, with the conscious thought of maintaining the balance of energy that is vital to the earth's existence.

G: Anisha, I have felt that for a while now, the need to generate *Light* to maintain balance. I can see how twin flames have a unique power to do so; two joined as one having a unique power. I do understand!

Anisha: I know you do. Once this concept is processed by the mind it is not difficult at all to understand. There is strength in unity. It is from a consciousness of this concept, of strength in unity, that the twins might consider remaining united in this moment.

Now, I will address your second question. You have asked how twin flames recognize each other, and how a twin flame differs from a soul mate. The answer is simple to state, yet it may be difficult to comprehend. The answer is simply that the souls know. When twins meet, they simply know. Those who are living this existence, who are sharing with their twin, understand this statement completely. They know and understand that the completion of their soul is being lived by the presence of each other's spirit.

But there is something I want you to understand. Twin flames do often live as couples. They may be husband and wife, lovers, close friends. Yet it is not necessary for twin flames to live together, only that they exist together. All that is necessary is for the souls to understand that they are one, that they are complete. How they choose to live and communicate will be their decision. Yet the consciousness will be present because twin flames understand their completion through a feeling in the soul. It is more than a feeling actually, it is a knowing.

G: I do understand what you are saying. However, how is this different from a soul mate? Don't soul mates share souls also?

Anisha: You are very kind, G. You ask questions for those who might not understand. You understand my message but are thinking of others who might not.

G: You're making me blush, Anisha.

Anisha: I am merely being sincere. I will answer the question. You see, soul mates recognize each other by a feeling from within the soul also. All matters of soul are recognized within the soul. But the difference between a soul mate and a twin flame is this. When one is sharing with a soul mate, feeling quite fine and content, there is still a yearning inside of itself that seeks to be completed. Please don't mistake this as a yearning to seek and explore matters of soul and the universe, to expand one's experiences and knowledge of the Creator's energy. This occurs within twin flames as well. Seeking higher levels of enlightenment is natural to all souls. But twin flames no longer feel a yearning to feel complete within them. They simply know they are complete.

Soul mates share so much with one another. They enrich each other. They guide, protect, support, and encourage one another. They help each other in so many ways. Yet even though soul mates share so much with each other, there is the absence of the feeling of completion. It is this unmistakable feeling of being complete, the actual knowing from one's inner knower, that is the difference between a soul mate and a twin flame.

I would love to offer a more detailed explanation, but the truth being what it is, I cannot. My suggestion to all who are interested in understanding this concept is to look within one's soul. Know and understand your soul. Take time to nurture your soul. For life truly is a journey of the soul, and ultimately all souls come to understand this truth. And in this understanding you will know, you will simply know.

G: I realize many would expect a more detailed explanation Anisha. You've made it quite simple.

Anisha: It is quite simple, G. All one must do is look into the soul.

G: I have another question. Can we call twin flames into our lives?

Anisha: Yes, you can. You can call your twin flame in a number of ways. You can pray, you can visualize, you can meditate. There will be a time when the soul calls out to its twin, calling him or her home. The call will be heard, and the twin will respond. It might not be in the immediate moment but the twin will hear and respond. Twins are joined, they are one. A twin cannot resist the call of its completion.

G: Everything you describe sounds so simple. Yet why do people struggle to find their twin, or even their soul mate?

Anisha: It is because they are not fully ready to accept such a relationship. Perhaps in their head and heart they are, but not in the soul. Each soul is an individual part of the great energy; each soul has a journey to travel. When the soul surrenders to the energy of spirit, it moves toward enlightenment. And it is in this moment of the journey, this conscious calling of the soul, that matters of soul are addressed and delivered. To participate in this energy, one must place himself within it. Many struggles arise because individuals neglect their souls. Many mistake the body and mind as the vehicles toward attracting their soul mate. Yet it is the soul that does the attracting. Hence the words *soul mate*!

Anisha

Life on earth is not a simple existence. It is an opportunity to discover one's true self, an opportunity to discover the depth of one's soul. It is an opportunity to realize that all of life is spirit and that spirit exists in all realms of creation. There are many distractions rendered by living as a human. Life on earth is to be considered a unique opportunity because each soul is offered an individual choice to either accept or reject the concept of spirit and spiritual energy. When an individual is ready to accept the world of spirit, then the soul becomes empowered and in this empowered state, issues of soul are addressed. So in reality it is quite simple. Find your soul and you will find your mates and perhaps your twin. There is an incredible power in discovering one's soul, and all one must do to find it is seek. It's so simple, G, so basic. All one must do is seek! Simply knock and allow spirit to know that you are ready to accept it. The door will open and an amazing journey will begin!

G: Anisha, I have enjoyed working with you so much! You are so light yet so deep as well. You have made me smile during the entire course of the interview. I'm so happy that you stayed with me, even through our respite of eight months.

Anisha: It has been my pleasure, G. You understand love and I love love. It's a perfect fit!

G: Sure is! Now, as all spirits do, it's time for you to render one final insight. I'm guessing what yours will be!

Anisha: You are clever, G! My final insight is one of simplicity. Just open your heart to spirit and open your heart to love. Love is the truest power of the universe. It transcends all realms of creation, it exists everywhere. Open your heart to love, believe in love, and love will work within you and through you. There is no magic in finding love but when you do find love, the entire world becomes magic! Love, love, love, then love some more. That's it, G. That's my final word, *love*. It's a good one!

G: Thank you so much, Anisha. You have filled me with love!

Anisha: Of course I have. That's my essence, silly! See ya!

G: Bye to you! And love to you, sooo much!

Anisha: Bye to you too, and love to you, soooo much so!

Ihon

Souls as Angels

Ihon is someone I truly did not expect to meet. He is a spirit that had never made himself known to me at any time before. He came to me suddenly and unexpectedly while on my usual Sunday sojourn to the beach. I was driving along the Robert Moses Causeway, heading toward Field 5 when his consciousness suddenly entered mine. He persisted in making himself felt, prodding me to listen to some new thoughts later as I was working out in the gym. He is interesting to me for a very special reason.

I don't wish to reveal too much about Ihon in this introductory paragraph. I will mention that he is here to speak about angels and what he has to say about them might surprise you. Then again, it might not! So, with no further explanation I introduce to you Ihon.

* * *

G: Welcome, Ihon. I certainly was surprised to hear from you.

Ihon: Hi, G. I know you were. I felt it when I entered your consciousness. It was a bit fun that way!

G: I'm sure it was. It was fun for me as well. I didn't know which spirit to expect next, and I didn't know that you would appear when you did. So, tell me about angels, do they really exist?

Ihon: Of course they do, and most people understand that they do. It's just the concept of how angels exist that might surprise a few readers.

G: Okay, no time for suspense. How will we be surprised by the existence of angels?

Ihon: Well I must first tell you that angels do exist. They exist in many forms and in all realms of the universe. The images of angels that most humans hold in their minds are true. Angels are a beautiful art form and messengers of the universe. They protect and guide one when they are called upon. That is not difficult to understand. There are so many wonderful stories of angels that exist, both in modern and ancient times.

Angels thrive on helping. It is their nature to serve the power of the Creator, the energy of love. They are tireless in their devotion to those they serve, for in service they understand that they are perpetuating light, and in doing so are serving the good of all of creation. All beings that exist in an enlightened state of consciousness come to understand that all of life is part of the total realm of creation. By serving the light, angels realize that they are assisting not just one individual, but all of creation. Angels are very real beings and do await your call.

G: I have long ago acknowledged the existence of angels. I have relied upon and communicated with my guardian angel since I was a small child. I still do. Would you kindly explain the concept of guardian angels?

Ihon: I'll try. You see, all angels are different in their nature. I am not a guardian angel; I am an angel of different sorts. For those who are familiar with Western medicine, try this analogy. There are many different doctors in Western society. An internist is quite different from a cardiologist, who in turn is quite different from a podiatrist. All are doctors and all have a basic knowledge of the human body, but if your heart were failing, you certainly would not visit a foot doctor! Keep this analogy in mind as I answer questions about angels.

With that said, yes, you do have a guardian angel; we all do. You have an awareness of him in your personal life and you can explain guardians as well as I can. Don't forget, you are a spirit as well. All humans are spirits, actually. It's just that many do not realize that they are and become enamored with spirits that exist beyond earth. Should humans begin to relax their minds and take time to explore their spirits, then they would come to understand this concept. Many already do. Guardians are wonderful angels that will stand by you through thick and thin. It is their cosmic job and joy to watch over you. They are ever present and will make themselves known to you whenever you need them. All you have to do is call. That's it. Like most things in the world of spirit, calling an angel is so simple. People have a tendency to make spirit so complex and mysterious. They are constantly looking outside of themselves, seeking the advice of others who profess a mystical link to the world of spirit, rather than going inside of their selves to find their truth. By going inside one learns to get outside. That is not a riddle but a truth. The world of spirit, the Kingdom of Heaven is within, not without. I will explain this concept further along in this interview. For now suffice it to say that you do have a guardian angel and this angel is waiting patiently for you. Just give him or her a call, and you will understand. Make it easy to manifest in your life; don't look for complications.

G: I'm sensing that you would like to explain the type of angel that you are, your "specialty", so to speak!

Ihon: You're correct, G. I would like to explain my specialty. Part of the explanation will be quite understandable, while part of it might be difficult to conceive. But one must understand that the world of spirit is so immense and so many dimensions exist! The human mind harbors the potential to understand dimensions that exist beyond the five senses and three dimensions that surround them. Just try to elevate your consciousness and consider the possibility of what I am about to explain.

Yes, I am an angel, but I am a human as well. That is a strange concept to some, a natural one to others. How does that sit with you?

G: To be quite honest, it sits very well in one way, but a bit strange in another. I do understand that people act as angels to one another, but how is it that you are a human and communicating with me through spirit?

Thon: That is a legitimate question, and I will respond. To begin, humans do act as angels to one another all the time. Many times, or even most times, the humans who are acting as angels don't even realize that they are doing so. How many times has a friend had the urge to call another that was feeling stress and needed a shoulder to lean on? How many times has someone come to the aid of another in distress? How many times has someone heard a conversation that someone was expressing confusion or despair, and interjected a bit of wisdom that helped this person gain a helpful insight? The answer is many, many times. It's happened to you, both on the giving and receiving end throughout your lifetime. It happens to us all.

When this happens, one is serving as an angel. Now it might not seem so to the reader at this point in time. But the truth is when one offers comfort to another then he or she is acting as an angel. The trick is to understand that a force of energy that is divine in nature has facilitated the act of compassion. This divine force of energy is the energy of love. Because of the fact that man is spirit in human form, he is receiving divine intervention in the form of feelings of compassion. Although this might be an unconscious kind of knowing, it is an energy that exists and is quite real. We are angels, G, each of us existing in human form. We are a certain kind of angel, and as humans we should recognize this. The next time you feel compelled to comfort someone who is in need, recognize that your kindness and compassion are divine.

G: That sounds so simple, Ihon. I have thought of that before. I believe you!

Ihon: All of spirit is simple, G. That is because all of life is spirit. Spirit is a natural way for all to exist. It's the human ego that separates one from the natural state of existence. Spirits before me have explained how ego affects the human condition. I don't have to elaborate on that. Just keep in mind that we all are capable of accessing the Divine because we all exist in the Divine. Just look at life through your soul, and it is easy to comprehend.

G: Thank you, Ihon. At this point in time, after communicating with the other spirits, I can understand that quite easily. Now, you had mentioned that you are human but an angel as well. Would you kindly elaborate on this concept?

Ihon: Certainly, but you must listen with your soul and an open mind. That is crucial if you are to understand this concept.

G: I will do so.

Ihon: Good, then I will begin. You see, I have just mentioned that we as humans do not always see beyond the five senses and three dimensions. The way the physical world is structured, it is not necessary to do so for survival. However, consider this. Should a human lose one of his senses, then his other senses will become more acute. A blind man's sense of smell, touch, taste, and hearing will become heightened because of his inability to see. Also, both the worlds of science and spirit seek discoveries of dimensions beyond the three that we see each day. There are many that profess that we use only a small portion of our brain's capacity and fail to capture its full potential. All these concepts are not foreign to you, or to most who will be reading this book.

The concepts stated above are true. There exist many dimensions beyond those that we know on earth! There are so many dimensions! Each dimension exists in its own vibration of energy, yet each dimension is an integral part of all of creation. Your question will be, is it possible to access other dimensions, to actually communicate with those of dimensions beyond those of earth? Am I correct?

G: You certainly are! I am fascinated by this concept. I've felt this is possible for so very long! Will you please elaborate?

Ihon: I will. You see, as humans we are composed of molecules of atoms that form our human bodies and our human brains. We share a similar composition and vibrate at a similar frequency. That is why we are visible to one another. That is why we relate to one another. It is a matter of frequency of vibration. However, there are those of the human race whose frequencies of vibration become sensitized to vibrations of dimensions beyond those of the human condition. We all possess this potential to do so; it's just that many of us do not feel the need to do so. Surviving in the human condition is a difficult chore. Many do not take the time to explore other frequencies. However, should one take the initiative to seek to discover other frequencies, then he or she will access dimensions of those beyond that of earth. This is not difficult, nor is it mystical. It is a matter of sensitizing one's vibration to the frequency of another dimension.

Try to consider this concept. We are all composed of energy; everything in the universe is made up of energy. Thus, we are truly energetic beings. Our thoughts are also expressions of energy; so thoughts actually become things. There exists in the universe a Great Energy, a collection of energy. I am comfortable describing the Great Energy with the term *superconscious*. Imagine, if you will, a great atmosphere of energy that contains collective thoughts. In this energy exists the collective energy of the entire universe. It is a vast energy and infinite in its possibility. In this energy one can find solutions to all of life's problems. In this energy man has made his greatest discoveries. Things truly have not been invented; rather they have been discovered. All technology already exists; it merely needs to be discovered. In this superconscious exists the universal mind of both the scientist and the artist. In this superconscious exists the mind of both the intellect and the spiritualist.

Once people discover this energy, then they may access it in any way that is natural to them, and as often as they wish. They may explore as many frequencies as they desire, or they may dwell in only one or a few of its vibrations. Obviously, the more time spent in one area, the more they will access that particular energy. One may become a "specialist", so to speak.

There are many ways to discover the superconscious. How an individual does so is unique to each of us who endeavors

Ihon

to do so. To return to the question you have asked, which is the kind of angel I am? It is from my journey into this vast superconscious that I have learned how to do what I do. And anyone can accomplish this; it's merely a matter of attention and persistence.

I have much to share with you regarding angels and the function of angels. My individual story is this. I exist in human form. I have long been a student of spirit, and in my discoveries I have been guided toward certain energy of the superconscious mind. In my personal discovery, I have learned to listen to the minds of others that are human and to offer assistance through thoughts. I do understand that this sounds incomprehensible to many who will read this, yet quite comprehensible to many who read this as well. A case in point is that I have heard your thoughts and have responded to you through mine. You have subsequently heard my reply and have been listening to me since that moment.

I have achieved a certain level of mastery regarding my ability to communicate on what might be termed a telepathic level. There have been many masters, masters far greater than me, who have learned to do this, and more. One needs only to look to the renowned prophets of time to understand this concept. One might also look toward the scientist, the artist, and the musician as well. The human race has hosted many, many masters over the course of time. Each master has learned in his and her own way to access the power of the superconscious energy that avails itself to one and all.

G: That is a fascinating concept, Ihon! It truly is! I understand this completely. I cannot explain it as explicitly as you have done, but I do understand!

Ihon: Of course you do. Are we not communicating at this very moment? I also know you will be curious, since I have revealed myself as existing as a human, who I might be.

G: To be honest, I do not seek your human identity. I prefer to communicate with you as a spirit.

Ihon: That is a wise decision. And by the way, G, you are dwelling in the superconscious energy yourself. You have met me here!

G: I understand this also. Having established this, would you please offer me and the readers a few insights more that you have to share?

Ihon: It is my pleasure to do so. I will address you through myself as an angel.

Angels do exist, G. They, or we, are entities that are quite real. I've mentioned earlier that there are many forms of angels. Angels abound in energies ranging from the etheric right down through the physical form of the human being. There are so many angels present in the universe! Yet no matter what form they exist in, their role is the same. Their role is to be of service. And all one need do to acquire their service is call. That is all one must do to solicit an angel!

G: That sounds so simple!

Ihon: Oh, G, it is that simple! The problem many people have is that when they call, they do not believe. Another problem is that many people envision angels to fly trumpeting from the sky, making a grandiose appearance. Angels are much subtler. They are most easily recognized when one relaxes and listens. Angels do manifest themselves in the flesh, yet they also make their presence known in more subtle ways. They may guide one toward a book, a song, a conversation, any number of subtle cues. Yet angels abound in the universe and await each individual's call. It is a very simple but powerful fact of the universe.

G: Ihon, each spirit before you has stressed the simplicity of accessing spirit. If this is so, why don't we all realize this on a conscious level?

Ihon: There are many people on the planet, so there are many reasons. You see, life is an individual adventure, an individual journey. There are many factors that shape one's perceptions. Environment, genetics, circumstances, these all contribute to an individual's perception of what life means. Yet in truth each individual has his or her own individual perception of reality. Some people make life very complicated. Some people's circumstances make life very complicated. However, complications are not true reasons to ignore the call to spirit. They are certainly distractions, but they are not valid reasons. And contrary to this, complications many times accelerate an individual's desire to find spirit. There are so many reasons why each individual on this planet decides to accept or decline the energy of spirit. But there is one certainty available to everyone. When one calls, spirit responds. It is an immutable law of the universe.

Now I understand that you will be asking for examples of how to call spirit and what one might expect. You will also be asking how one can access different vibrations, different frequencies of vibration. Am I correct?

G: Of course you are! That is a reasonable request at this time, don't you agree?

Ihon: Yes, I do. Once again, making the call is quite simple. All one has to do is call. One may use formal prayer, or one may speak plainly from the heart. The words are not particularly significant; it is the faith of one's heart that makes the connection. If prayers or requests are empty, if they are demands, or if they are said with no belief at all, then spirit will not respond. But when the heart calls, even if the words are hard, spirit will respond. The reason for this is that spirit is the energy of love. And love has no concrete definition; it is an individual concept. Love is a vast and powerful energy, and when one calls from the heart, calls from love, then love responds.

Many individuals make the mistake of expecting prayers to be answered instantly. Many want to know now, the moment the call is made. Spirit sometimes responds in that manner, sometimes not. Once the call is made, spirit will respond as the heart opens to hear it. Spirit does not open and close its energy. It is available in all moments. It is the individual who opens and closes the heart. Spirit does not run away from an individual, it is ever present. Spirit will not feel rejected when one moves away from its presence. It will be there when one returns to its presence. Spirit exists in all moments.

I have mentioned that there exists a great energy, a super-conscious energy that contains all the energies of the universe within it. People may access this energy in any way their heart leads them. They may sensitize their vibration to an infinite number of frequencies that exist. This is how they access what some call psychic energy. They merely sensitize their vibration to that of the psychic dimension. Spirits before me have used the following analogy, yet it is worth repeating once more. All one must do is become aware of all the frequencies of vibration existing in the world of communication.

There are radio stations and television stations broadcasting on different bands of frequency throughout earth's atmosphere. Satellite transmission has increased the availability of accessing broadcasts from every corner of the earth. Yet even though so many broadcasts exist simultaneously and are available to so many, many are never heard, for they are never explored. But should one be tuning the dial and suddenly discover a station new to them, then they suddenly receive a new perspective, a new energy. They are then free to immerse themselves in this newfound energy, they may move past it or visit it as they feel the desire or need to do so. When they move past that frequency, it still exists. When they return it will still be there. Of course formats are sometimes changed and a new energy will then occupy that frequency. So it is with the energy of spirit. The universe is not stagnant; it is ever changing and evolving. Humans are ever changing and evolving as well.

The same is true for technology. Yet the one constant energy in all of creation is the energy of *Love*. And the one constant condition in the human existence is the presence of soul. Love will always be *Love*, and soul will always be soul.

You are no doubt now desiring an explanation of how to contact angels and how angels will respond. This is the area I've come forward to address.

I have stated previously that the role of all angels is assistance. Angels have been created and thrive on helping any soul who calls upon them! There are so many angels. There is literally an angel for every soul that exists! And the beauty of it all is that all one has to do is call from the heart. I've also stated before that there are different kinds of angels and that each soul is itself an angel. I believe that is a simple concept to understand. I have also mentioned that even as I am now existing as a human being, I am also an active angel. I will explain my experience, hoping that others will explore their own potential to answer their call!

As a human being, I am quite ordinary. My life is rather conventional. I need not describe the details of my human existence. My path toward discovery has been a life's journey. Since a child I have felt the presence of spirit. I was unable to define my feelings and intuitions as a child, but I was always aware of the presence of spirit. Being unable to define this, I did not explore it deeply. There were many conventional influences on my life that turned me away from spiritual exploration, yet the inner knowing always existed. As time went on and my life's experiences allowed me to discover different perspectives, my spiritual curiosity became greatly aroused. I began to trust my intuitions, even though they contradicted the

Ihon

circumstances and lifestyle I had been living. It was difficult in ways for me to express my thoughts and feelings because those who I was journeying with mocked them. So I learned to turn inward and make my discoveries privately and discreetly. I learned how to seek the world of spirit in a very personal way. I read many books, listened to many speakers, spent many moments in meditation. I observed the ways of nature. I sought spirit with a very open mind and learned to use the ideas that felt comfortable to me, and to discard those that felt uncomfortable. I learned to listen more than speak and, for me, that was the key to my spiritual evolution. Through patience, persistence, and faith I have evolved to the place in which I now dwell. I have sensitized myself to this particular vibration, and this is how I have learned to communicate with others through the mind.

I realize to many this will sound like pure rubbish, pure folly. I do understand this is difficult for many to believe. However, I also understand that there are many who are reading this who do share my experience, or at least have a feeling inside of their soul that they too can learn to access different frequencies of vibration. Learning to do so is not something mystical—it is not magic. It is merely seeking to understand life through the spirit and the soul. All it takes is some time and faith!

As an angel who exists in the realm that I do, I listen for the call of souls who are seeking guidance. That is how I met you, G. Our minds have met each other. You can even recall the exact moment and circumstance! And I must tell you that your excitement was not yours alone. My excitement was equally as strong! As an angel it is my true pleasure to be of service. And another thought to bear in mind is this. I am not unique to this dimension. There are many, many angels like myself. And there will be many, many more. Life is a process that continues. Life is an ever-evolving journey.

Now, how do angels of my dimension assist others? There are numerous ways. My way is to subtly guide souls toward discovering the answers to the questions they seek. There are many that are trying to unlock the secrets and mysteries of spiritual existence and actively seek answers to their questions. Of course I try to convey to them that there are no real secrets and mysteries. Those who would have you believe in secrets and mysteries are those who seek to empower themselves and often times control others. There are no secrets and mysteries in the realm of spirit; only truth exists. And one basic truth is that all of life, in every dimension, in all of creation, is spirit. And an equally great truth is that the greatest of all energies is the energy of love!

Think of yourself in your teaching career, G. You have served as an angel to so many! In each child you have worked with, you have always seen his or her light. You have seen in each child his or her unique intelligence, you have seen in each and every child his or her potential to succeed. You have helped each and every child believe in him- or herself at some level. You did so in an effortless way, in a way that all who knew you recognized as genuine. And, G, your inner knower was always aware that this was the result of a divine energy that was moving though you. You had simply accessed an energy that is divine because you saw each child through the eyes of love.

G: Thanks. Ihon. Thanks for your kind words. I've always known it was so. I could not really explain it, but I just knew.

Ihon: Yes, G, I'm aware of this. You accessed a very powerful energy that was channeled through love. The truth is, all who exist have access to this energy. Of course each soul is unique, so each manifestation of the energy will be unique, yet it is all the same. The energies of light and love are available to us all, in our own special way. And once we understand this, once we feel this within our inner knower, then we become capable of accessing this energy on a regular basis. Because we all have the potential to access the Divine, we all have the potential to act as angels. This is not a difficult concept to understand, nor is it a difficult task to accomplish. This is best understood through a mind that is open and relaxed, rather than through a mind that is straining to find some mystical truth. All one needs to do is relax and listen to his or her soul. All one needs to do is listen to love.

G: Once again, Ihon, that does sound simple. Do you have any specific methods to offer those who are entertaining your insights?

Ihon: Yes, G, use the tools that are most natural to you. Use the tools that feel right. Trust your intuition, trust the part of you that needs not analyze or evaluate, trust the part of you that simply knows.

G: What are the "tools" you refer to?

Ihon: One's greatest tool is his or her intuition. One simple way to learn to enhance this tool of intuition is to learn to listen. There are many methods of doing so. Try a walk along the beach, a walk in the woods. Listen to the birds, spend some time observing the beauty of flowers. Pray, meditate, listen to soothing music. There are so many ways to find a quiet place in your mind. It is in this quiet place that one learns to hear the voice of spirit. It is really not an internal dialogue that one hears—it is the feeling of knowing that one learns to hear. Spend some time discovering what resonates most powerfully within you. Then all you need to do is listen to your spirit and trust what you hear.

G: Ihon, what about people who listen to things they hear and use this "voice," so to speak, to commit acts of violence or hatred?

Ihon: This is an honest question, and I will address it in the best manner that I can.

G, there is a distinct feeling that peace offers us. When one experiences a feeling of peace, then one experiences the energy of love. There is no hatred within love; there is no violence or discord. People know when they are feeling love, they simply know. Any thoughts that move away from love cannot produce the feeling that love delivers to the body. Response to hatred and violence produces a feeling, or energy, this is distant from peace.

When peace exists it is unmistakable. It is a feeling that cannot be defined by words; it is an energy defined by feeling. We might be able to deceive our cognitive mind through words and images, but a violent mind cannot deceive one's spirit, one's soul.

A violent mind is never at peace. Only a peaceful mind can be at peace. If you take a moment to consider this thought, you will understand that anything perceived outside of peace is a voice removed from love. The voice of love is unmistakable. You need not hear it with your ears; you hear it though a feeling in your soul.

G: Thank you, Ihon. I do understand. Do you think those who are reading this will understand this as well?

Ihon: They will if they are ready. Those who are walking the path toward enlightenment, those who are seeking truth inside their hearts will understand this thought completely.

G: Thank you, Ihon. I thank you for all you have shared with us. I am very grateful that you have entered my consciousness. I have come to know you as my true and valued friend.

Ihon: And I have come to know you as my friend as well.

G: Ihon, it is time to ask you for a closing thought, a final insight to offer those who have met you!

Ihon: It is my pleasure, G.

I would like everyone to understand that angels are real; they abound in the universe. Keep in mind that angels thrive on helping—it is the nature of who they are. In any moment, in any circumstance, all one must do to access an angel is simply make the call and believe it is heard. Faith is so important. Believe in an angel's intervention, and it will be delivered to you.

Communicate often with your guardian angel. He or she surrounds you with love and is always present to offer you guidance. Trust your intuition, and you will feel your guardian angel's presence.

Finally, keep in mind that we all are angels to one another. Acts of kindness, understanding, and compassion are divine interventions we are all capable of delivering. Trust your spirit and your soul, for your angelic character exists within you always.

G: Thank you, Ihon. Thank you for all you have shared. You truly are an angel. You truly are a very special soul.

Ihon: You are as well, G. We all are. I wish you all peace, love, and a smile in your heart! Give an angel a call…they can't wait to hear from you!

Glennisms

Simple Thoughts About Life & Living
The Thought For The Day
was created with YOU in mind!

Sometimes a single perception can open a pathway in your consciousness to help set in motion a wanted change in your life; other times a perception might help to reinforce a knowing that you already possess. There are also times when a perception might move you to help someone in need. And there are times when a perception might simply make you smile.

It is my hope that these thoughts might help to uplift some people. I hope that these uplifted people will help others to feel uplifted, and they in turn will help others. It can be done with just a few simple thoughts; that's all it really takes.

Thoughts For The Day are sent each Monday, Wednesday, and Friday. To receive yours visit www.thepov.net. Go to the top and click on Newsletter, then register your screen name. It's free!

Kindness is one of the simplest, yet most powerful, gifts that you can either give or receive. I hope kindness will be a part of your day!

We each have X amount of breaths to take in life; X amount of steps to take; X amount of days to dance. Try not to waste any dancing days complaining about things that won't matter at all once your dancing days are through!

Life is simply how you look at it; it's what you perceive it to be. Once you learn to look at it in ways that make your existence happy then I think you discover the secret to life. It takes some practice to shift perspectives, but it's well worth the time and energy you'll spend on doing so!

People can inspire faith in you; stay close to those who do so. But the faith that will allow you to move mountains is the faith that you have in yourself. Think about that!

Having a lot of money in the bank makes life a whole lot easier; it sure feels good! But it won't necessarily fill one's heart with peace. The wealthiest of all people in life are the ones whose hearts are filled with peace and who are truly at ease with themselves.

Here's an interesting thought about the power of faith: The world tells us, "Prove it...seeing is believing." But faith works just the opposite. Faith tells us, "If you believe first, then you will see it."
Think about that!

We gain peace when we surrender our anxiety. If troubling thoughts are causing anxious moments for you, surrender those thoughts to different thoughts that make you feel better. This will empower you and offer you the peace that each of us deserves. Think about that!

There are many people in life who accomplish so much more than others think they are capable of accomplishing These special people are often labeled overachievers. That is not the truth. They are not over achievers, what they really are is fervent believers. They see themselves achieving and believe with all their heart that they will. And that's why they do so!

Life can be fragile; it can change in the blink of an eye. That's why it is so important to appreciate all that is good while it is good. Another reason to be aware of your blessings is that the more you count them, the more you appreciate them…..the more you will attract into your life.

If you really, really DESIRE something, and you really, really can see yourself having or being it, and you really, really BELIEVE that you can,….. then you already do because your feet are on the path. Think about that….it's powerful!

Both the daydreamer and the person who accomplishes things have many creative thoughts and visions. The difference between the two is that the person who accomplishes things takes action—the daydreamer simply moves on to the next lofty dream.

Author's Note

I would like to add a few personal insights to this work. Being a conduit of the spirits' energy has been such a rewarding and fascinating experience for me. I will begin by offering my sincere thanks to each special spirit who has shared his and her story with me in hopes that they might somehow help you.

Thank you Billy and Haddie, Haitukulu, Chief, Mamma Soul, Angel of Zarton, Anisha, and Ihon. I have learned so much from you. I am so very grateful for being chosen to share your energy with the world.

Your lessons have left an indelible impression on my mind and soul. I have learned from you that we are all spirit, each and every one of us. We are all a part of one, great energy which is the energy of the Creator; the energy of Love. We are free to attune ourselves to this energy at any moment in time. It is simply a matter of choosing to do so.

You have all helped to reinforce a knowing that I've had since I was a child. This knowing is about faith, about trusting our inner knower. It is the part of each of us that needs no explanation of the presence of spirit; it is something we simply know. This inner knower is the part of our soul that guides us toward the Creator's energy and is available to us at all moments in time. It will not seek us; it simply awaits our call. All we need do is knock, and the call will be answered. I truly believe this to be an immutable law of the universe.

My final statement reflects the truth that is told by each of these wonderful entities. The most powerful of all energies is the energy of Love. The more we learn to open our minds and hearts to this energy, the more it will fill us, guide us, and strengthen us. As we become immersed in the energy of Love we learn to become less centered in ourselves and more open to the understanding that whatever good we do is for the highest good of all of creation.

As each spirit has done, I will make one concluding statement, a statement short and sweet:

I wish you Love....

Purchase Information Page

For more information regarding
Mr. Glenn Poveromo and his work
contact him at **creatingstrength@aol.com**
or visit his Web site
www.thepov.net

Further copies of this book may be purchased
from your favorite bookstore
or online via AuthorHouse.com, Amazon.com,
BarnesAndNoble.com, Borders.com.